A Baghdad Cookery Book

Petits Propos Culinaires 79

Petits Propos Culinaires 79

A Baghdad Cookery Book

THE BOOK OF DISHES (*Kitāb al-Ṭabīkh*)

Muḥammad b. al-Ḥasan b. Muḥammad b. al-Karīm,
the scribe of Baghdad

Newly Translated by Charles Perry

Prospect Books November 2005

THE COVER ILLUSTRATION is by Marion V. Dorn. It is one of her illustrations to the Nonesuch Press edition of William Beckford's *Vathek*, published in 1929.

First published in Great Britain in 2005 as an independent title and as a special issue, PPC 79, of the journal *Petits Propos Culinaires* by Prospect Books, 26 Parke Road, London, SW13 9NG.

Reprinted 2017, 2021, 2022.

As an independent title: ISBN 978-1-903-018-42-2
As an issue of *PPC*: ISSN 0142-4857

Typeset in Jaghbub by Ben Morrow and Tom Jaine.

Printed and bound in Great Britain by the Gutenberg Press, Malta..

TABLE OF CONTENTS

Mishmishiyya
Nāranjiyya
Nārsūn
Maṣūṣiyya
Al-Maḍīra
Buqūliyya
Labaniyya
Buqūliyya [Mukarrara]
Mujazzaᶜa
ᶜUkaika
Maṣliyya

Chapter II: on plain dishes according to [their variety] 45
Isfānākhiyya
Rukhāmiyya
Āruzz Mufalfal
Shūrbā
Mujaddara
Iṭriya
Rāshtā
ᶜAdasiyya
Ḥinṭiyya
Farīkiyya
Muhallabiyya, which is called al-bihaṭṭa
Isfīdhabāja
Sughdiyya
Shūrbā Khaḍrāᵓ
Māᵓ wa-Ḥimmaṣ
Māᵓ al-Bāqillā
Māsh
Mulabbaqa

Māliḥ Maqlū Sādhij
Māliḥ Mukazbar
Māliḥ bi-Khall wa-Khardal
Maqlūbat al-Ṭarrīkh
Mufarraka
Ṭarrīkh Maḥsī

Chapter VII: On pickles, relishes and condiments 86
Na^{c}na^c Mukhallal
Bādhinjān Mukhallal
Lift Mukhallal Muḥallā
Bādhinjān Maḥsī
Bādhinjān bi-Laban
Qar^c bi-Laban
Silq bi-Laban
Shīrāz bi-Buqūl
Isfānākh Muṭajjan
Kāmakh Rījāl
Zaitūn Mubakhkhar
Khall wa-Khardal
Milḥ Muṭayyab
Bāqillā bi-Khall

Chapter VIII: *Jūdhābs*, puddings and what is analogous to them 92
Jūdhāb al-Khubz
Jūdhāb al-Qatayif
Jūdhāb Khubz al-Qaṭayif
Jūdhāb al-Khashkhāsh
Jūdhāb Khabīṣ al-Lauz
Jūdhāb al-Tamr
Jūdhāb al-Ruṭab
Sifat jūdhāb ākhar

Ṣifat Khabīṣ
Ṣifa ukhrā
Ṣifa ukhrā
Khabīṣ al-Lauz
*Khabīṣ al-Qar*ᶜ
Khabīṣ al-Jazar

Chapter IX: Mentioning sweetmeats and their varieties of that (sort) 98
Ḥalwā Yābisa
Ṣābūniyya
Fustuqiyya
Makshūfa
Lauzīnaj
Fālūdhaj
Mukaffan
Barad
Samak wa-Aqrāṣ

Chapter X: On making *khushkanānaj*, *mutbaq*, crepes and things mixed with flour that are analogous to those 102
Khushkanānaj
Muṭbaq
Urnīn wa-Khubz al-Abāzīr
Aqrāṣ Mukallala
Qaṭāyif
Aqrāṣ Mukarrara
Faṭāyir
Mubaḥthara
Luqam al-Qāḍī
*Ruṭab Mu*ᶜ*assal*
Ṣifat ᶜ*amal ruṭab fī ghair awānihi*
Ḥais

INTRODUCTION

Kitāb al-Ṭabīkh, composed by a thirteenth-century scribe we usually call al-Baghdādī, was long the only medieval Arabic cookery book known to the English-speaking world, thanks to A.J. Arberry's path-breaking 1939 translation as 'A Baghdad Cookery Book' (reissued by Prospect Books in 2001 in *Medieval Arab Cookery*).

For centuries, it had been the favourite Arabic cookery book of the Turks. The original manuscript, formerly held in the library of the Aya Sofya Mosque, is still in Istanbul; it is now MS Ayasofya 3710 in the Süleymaniye Library. At some point a Turkish sultan commissioned a very handsome copy, now MS Oriental 5099 in the British Library in London. At a still later time, a total of about 260 recipes were added to *Kitāb al-Ṭabīkh*'s original 160 and the expanded edition was retitled *Kitāb Waṣf al-Aṭ*^{c}*ima al-Mu*^{c}*tāda* (my translation of it also appears in *Medieval Arab Cookery*); three currently known copies of *K. Waṣf* survive, all in Turkey – two of them in the library of the Topkapi Palace, showing the Turks' high regard for this book. Finally, in the late fifteenth century Şirvâni made a Turkish translation of *Kitāb al-Ṭabīkh*, to which he added some recipes current in his own day, thus creating the first Turkish cookery book.

As the pioneer translator of medieval Arabic recipes, young Arberry – later to be one of the twentieth century's most illustrious Middle East scholars – solved a number of problems presented by this text, but inevitably he got things wrong, and in *Medieval*

Arab Cookery I ventured to correct his translation on a few points. On closer examination, I have found many more mistakes, some of them rather shocking. They simply show that Arberry – like most academics, past and present – was interested in literature (his essay on food in medieval Arabic literature is an enduring classic), but not in cookery.

When I examined the original manuscript of *Kitāb al-Ṭabīkh* at the Süleymaniye Library last year, I was struck by the degree to which all students of this book, Arberry included, have been at the mercy of the published Arabic text produced by the Iraqi scholar Daoud Chelebi in 1934. As the first to study this book, Chelebi had solved a number of its problems (including, as he noted in his introduction, correcting al-Baghdadi's grammar at many points). But he had also made omissions and questionable readings. In Chelebi's defence, he was working at a time when Turkish libraries did not conveniently provide photocopies on computer disks. He'd been obliged to copy the text the medieval way, by hand, with all the opportunities for error which hand copying has always provided (there is a peculiar example in the **Samak wa-Aqrāṣ** recipe).

Far more seriously, Chelebi selected among the many marginal notes in the book purely on the basis of his own estimate of their value. Though he parenthesized nearly all the notes he chose that had been inserted from ibn Jazla's *Minhāj al-Bayān*, he also parenthesized some of al-Baghdādī's own marginal additions, while omitting others. As a result, the text Chelebi published was not really al-Baghdādī's, and Arberry made matters worse by leaving out the parentheses. Arberry's introductory note does not even acknowledge that there is marginal material.

I should say that the 1934 edition of *Kitāb al-Ṭabīkh* has been very rare for over half a century. I have only been able to inspect the reprint edited by Fakhri al-Barudi (Dar al-Kitab al-Jadid, Damascus, 1964), which evidently differs in some particulars.

Since 1934 other manuscripts derived from al-Baghdādī's original have come to light, and in general much more has been learned about medieval Arab cookery. Altogether, I feel it is time for a fresh translation of this important book from the original manuscript, explaining when it differs from the Arberry/Chelebi version.

THE TEXT

The book consists of 54 pages measuring 20 x 14 centimetres, with 15 lines of *naskhī* script to the page. Most vowels are written, but in some cases al-Baghdādī omits the vowel marks, or even the dots that distinguish certain consonants from others, apparently acknowledging that he is not sure how the passage should be read. With distressing frequency, he writes the dots that distinguish 'z' from 'r' and 'sh' from 's' where they don't belong. Where the London MS or *K. Waṣf* makes the meaning clear, I pass over most errors and ambiguities in silence.

After completing his manuscript, al-Baghdādī went over it and discovered that he had omitted words or even sentences, so he wrote them in the margins. I restore these omissions between brackets [ ] to indicate that they appear in the margin, but I do not bracket words that he merely wrote above a line or part way into the margin. (Any words that appear between parentheses ( ) are my own, and to emphasize this I sometimes precede them by 'i.e.' or 'sc.')

At a much later time (after page 9b-10a had been damaged and replaced by a copy in different hand), an unknown scribe added a great deal of material from the eleventh-century medical encyclopaedia *Minhāj al-Bayān* in the margins. Most of these additions concern the purported medical properties of the dishes, and I omit them. But others are of interest from a culinary standpoint.

The additions from *Minhāj* were evidently made after *Kitāb al-Ṭabīkh* had been copied and begun to circulate, because they don't appear in the London manuscript or the three manuscripts of *Kitāb Waṣf*. Strictly speaking, they are irrelevant to this book. Nevertheless I have translated them after the individual recipes where they appear: between quote marks, if the unknown scribe or Chelebi indicated that the material belonged within the recipe, or between brackets, if they seemed to consider it separate. In every case I indicate where it is material from *Minhāj*.

The book gives two recipes for *buqūliyya*. Al-Baghdādī wrote the word *mukarrara* ('repeated') in the margin next to the second one, and all subsequent copies of this manuscript, including the Arabic text published by Chelebi, have concluded that it merely repeats the first recipe. In fact, the two recipes are somewhat different, and al-Baghdādī intended *buqūliyya mukarrara* to be in the book, because he added a marginal note to it. I reproduce this second recipe here, apparently for the first time in history.

There are a few curious interlinear glosses in the first recipe, **Al-Sikbāj**. Persian glosses: *kurrāth* 'leek' as *gandaneh*, *jazar* 'carrot' as *gazar* and *kusfara khaḍrā* 'green coriander' as *gashniz-e ?yās* (second word obscure). Turkish glosses: *mighrafa* 'ladle' as *kepçeler* (ladles), *badhinj* 'eggplant' (wrongly) as *kuzu* 'lamb', *yuqashshar* 'is peeled' as *soyar*, *lauz muqashshar* 'peeled almonds' as *soyulmuṣ badem*, *dāfa fihi* 'it was mixed in it' as *isladi* 'it was wetted', *yuslaq* 'is boiled' as *kaynadılar* 'they boiled it' and *raghwatuhu* 'its scum' as *köpüğü*; the puzzling gloss of *yasīr ᶜunnab* 'a few jujubes' might be read *az min ünnabi*, an odd mixture of Turkish and Arabic. In Arabic, *tahdaᵓ ᶜalā ḥummā al-nār* 'it grows quiet on the heat of the fire' is explained as *ay taskun ḥarāratuhu* 'that is, its heat abates' and *ghamruhu māᵓ* 'enough water to cover it' as *al-māᵓ ᶜalāhu* 'the water is higher than it'. Perhaps some scribe planned to gloss the whole book but then gave up, or perhaps he wanted to make the nature of this famous dish clear to any casual reader, with particular regard to a Turkish reader.

RECIPE TERMINOLOGY

Most stew recipes say to leave the pot on the fire 'until it becomes quiet'. It's often hard to tell whether this means 'until the pot becomes quiet' (that is, until the food has stopped boiling) or 'until the fire becomes quiet' (until it no longer flames and is reduced to embers). Both meanings of 'quiet' are expressed in the text. **Mudaqqaqāt Sādhija** (page 65) has: 'When it is done, cut the fire from it and leave it on a quiet fire awhile until it (the pot) becomes quiet'; and **Samak Mashwī** (page 81) has: 'a quiet fire, not flaming'.

Probably this is just a conventional instruction meaning 'simmer it until it is ready to serve'. (The recipe **Maṣūṣ** says to leave the dish on the fire 'until it grows quiet and its cooking is finished'.) Likewise, the recipes vacillate between 'the pot is left on the fire awhile until it grows quiet' and 'the pot is left on the fire until it grows quiet awhile', without any discernible difference in meaning. Nevertheless, I have translated such phrases literally.

Most chapters list dishes that are cooked or seasoned in one particular way. From this point of view, Chapter V reads like a hodgepodge. I suspect that what the dishes in Chapter V have in common is not a cooking method but the fact that they were eaten as snacks, like today's *meze*.

The verb *rabbā* (generally followed by the words *bil-mā*, 'with water') literally means 'to develop', but the real sense seems to be what we see in the modern Arabic verb *rabb*, 'to beat to liquid consistency' and I translate it with those words. It is applied only to pounding or grinding nuts and thinning them with a liquid.

When 'fingers' are used as a measurement, the meaning is the width of a finger. Measurement by finger-widths is used when cutting certain vegetables. It is also used to specify how high ingredients should stand in the pot. In *maghmūma*, for instance, solid ingredients are layered 'until they remain four or five finger-widths from (the bottom of) the pot' (*ḥattā yabqā arba*ᶜ *khams aṣābi*ᶜ *min al-qidr*), which I translate 'until they stand four or five finger-widths deep'.

The other possible interpretation – that four or five finger-widths of space remain between the surface of the ingredients and the rim of the pot – is implausible for two reasons. First, this sort of instruction is used when water is added to grain dishes such as *tannūriyya*, where the quantity of water is crucial and the amount of unused space in the pot is irrelevant. Second, stew pots were carved from soapstone and, to judge from the soapstone cookware of modern Yemen, would rarely have been deep enough to indulge in a lot of empty space.

The instruction to 'refine' (*yukhla*ᶜ) sesame oil seems to mean frying spices such as cumin and coriander in it. Chelebi proposed that 'refining' was done by boiling the oil in water and skimming. Sometimes oil was treated in this way, but that process was known as 'washing'.

The names of some ingredients, such as *bādhinjān*, 'eggplant', are collective nouns, and to indicate a single example the 'singulative' suffix *-a* is added. However, colloquial Arabic sometimes omits the suffix. To render this ambiguity I translate such words as collectives – that is, in the singular without an article – but when there are instructions to cut off the leaves and stem I use plural pronouns. (In recipes such as **Madfūna** and **Bādhinjān Mukhallal**, the sense of *bādhinjān* is definitely plural.)

When a number of spices are listed in a recipe, generally only the last one in the list is modified by the expression *madqūq* (*masḥūq*) *nā*ᶜ*iman*, 'finely pounded (ground)'. Sometimes the adjective is plural in form or contains a modifier such as *jamī*ᶜ*an* 'all' to emphasize that the description actually applies to all the spices, but usually the adjective is singular. I have rendered all such passages literally. Nevertheless, recipes such as **Nārsūn** make it clear that, as we should expect, all spices were ground unless the recipe explicitly says that they are added whole: coriander as seeds, cinnamon or ginger root as sticks.

Often the measurement 'one *dirham*' appears before a list of spices, leaving it uncertain whether it refers to a *dirham* of each spice separately or a *dirham* in total. **Ruṭabiyya** says to add 'about two and a half *dirhams* in all' of spices, which suggests the usual total quantity of spice in a recipe. Guided by this, I have suggested parenthetically how *dirham* should be read.

In **Ruṭabiyya**, dates are described as *gharīq*, 'drowned'. Elsewhere in Arab culinary literature, the sweetmeats *lauzīnaj* and *fālūdhaj* are said to be 'drowned' when they are stored in syrup. Possibly these dates were immersed in syrup to keep them from drying out and losing the luxurious texture of ultra-ripe dates (*ruṭab*), as dates are covered with honey in **Ruṭab Mu^{c}assal**. But since the dates called for in **Ruṭab Mu^{c}assal** are themselves described as *gharīq*, the exact sense may be 'suitable for drowning'.

The expression *ḥalqat shibitt*, 'ring of dill', refers to a bunch of dill; perhaps the stalks were tied in a ring or knot to make it easier to remove them when cooking was done. Dill is always removed before serving except in *mā' wa-himmaṣ* and *kabīs*. (**Isfīdhabāj** of chicken does not call for removing the dill, but it is a mere sketch of a recipe.) There does not seem to be any significant difference between *ḥalqat shibitt*, *ṭāqāt shibitt* ('bunches of dill') and *^{c}īdān shibitt* ('stalks of dill').

Sometimes spices are pounded (*madqūq*) in a mortar; at other times they are ground (*masḥūq*, *maṭḥūn*) on a flat stone. One recipe says that spices are 'ground' in a mortar, but the London MS corrects 'mortar' to 'stone'.

Dry mint is regularly rubbed between the hands over the pot as a final step. I translate this as 'crumble into the pot', rather than 'rub into the pot'.

In this manuscript, the word *dirham* (plural *darāhim*) is often abbreviated to *ham* (*him*) after numerals and the word *niṣf* (half).

Arberry rendered the term *afāwīh ṭayyiba*, literally 'good mouths', as 'aromatic herbs'. I suggest that the herbs may be fresh, because the 'mouths' are never ground.

The word *tawābil* generally means 'spices' in Arabic, but **Sikbāj Tannūrī** and **Qannabīṭiyya** make it clear that it could refer to vegetables. Like *tawābil*, *ḥawāyij* ('things, necessities') often means spices, but it might best be translated as 'flavourings', because sometimes, as in **Maghmūma**, it seems to refer to vegetables. *Aṭrāf al-ṭib* was the term for mixed spices; the general word for spices was *abāzīr*.

In this translation have left the word *dist* untranslated. It was a tinned copper tray with relatively high sides which could be set up over a fire (for making puddings or sweetmeats) or inserted under the roasting chicken in a tandoor oven (for holding *jūdhāb*).

The recipe *shīrāz bi-buqūl* makes it clear that *shīrāz* was different from yogurt thickened by draining it in a cloth overnight. In Ibn al-Sayyār's *Kitāb al-Ṭabīkh* (tenth century) and *Kitāb Zahr al-Ḥadīqa* (thirteenth or fourteenth century), the difference is that *shīrāz* is not only soured but thickened with rennet before draining it. In the tenth-century book, *laban māst* (*māst* being the Persian word for yogurt) was similar, except that the milk was simply left out until it soured, rather than being cultured with a starter, before rennet was added, and it was not drained.

The name of the dish **Muṭajjan** might suggest that it was fried in the copper pan *ṭājin*, but these recipes mention only the iron or soapstone frying pan *miqlā*. **Muṭajjan** is just the conventional name of a dish of meat (or eggs) fried and then flavoured with vinegar and soy sauce.

'Dainty' (*laṭīf*) meatballs appear in **Būrāniyya**, **Raiḥāniyya** and **Khuḍairiyya**. The intention seems to be to distinguish them from meatballs the size of oranges.

The dish *jūdhāb* consisted of chicken roasted in the tandoor oven, with a pudding (the *jūdhāb* proper) placed under it when its juices start to run. This was the most famous dish of the age, so recipes for *jūdhāb* do not always bother to mention inserting it in the tandoor.

In my earlier writings on this book and *K. Waṣf*, I have used Arberry's spelling of the word 'chicken' (*dujāj*), which approximates the modern colloquial pronunciation. However, this manuscript explicitly spells this word in the classical way (*dajāj*). At the risk of pointlessly confusing and irritating everybody, I have reverted to *dajāj*.

INGREDIENTS AND BATTERIE DE CUISINE

'Tail fat' refers to the Middle Eastern fat-tailed sheep, which have been bred to concentrate their body fat in their tails and rumps.

The type of orange known in the Middle Ages was the sour Seville orange, also known as the bitter orange.

Samīd, like semolina, was a wheat product finer than groats but coarser than flour. Because it might refer to a particular kind of wheat, I leave it untranslated. The term poppy seed meal (*samīd khashkhāshī*), which appears in the stew *khashkhāshiyya*, refers to poppy seed ground to the consistency of *samīd*, coarser than flour.

Balāṭa, a large tile used in paving floors, served as the equivalent of a pastry marble.

A new utensil appears to emerge in this translation: *miqlā al-maqlūba*, the *maqlūba* pan, a thin iron or copper pan for frying patties of meat or fish bound with eggs.

Approximate values of the weights and measures: 1 pound (*raṭl*): 400 grams; 1 ounce (*ūqiya*): 33 grams; 1 *dīnār*: 4.25 grams; 1 *dirham*: 3 grams; 1 *rub*ᶜ (a quarter of a measure called *qadaḥ*): 23.5 decilitres, about 1 American measuring cup; 1 *dānaq*: 0.5 gram.

For a more complete discussion of the medieval Arab kitchen see *Medieval Arab Cookery*.

Charles Perry

The Book of Dishes

by

Muhammad b. al-Hasan b. Muhammad b. al-Karīm,
the scribe of Baghdad,

may God forgive him.

In the name of God, the Merciful, the Compassionate, in whom is (our) trust and aid. Praised be God, the creator of days and appointer of times, the resurrector of mankind, the cause of foods, the creator of animals, who with His manifest blessings causes the plants to grow which encompass the land. For them (i.e., mankind) He sends down water from heaven, and with it He causes (all) of the fruits to emerge. He has made good things lawful for them and permitted foods and drinks, except for the forbidden kinds. God bless His prophet and chosen one, Muhammad, and his family, and bring him to the highest degrees; indeed, He is the Hearer of prayers.

Now, God – exalted be He – made the good kinds of food lawful and permitted the enjoyment of them: those which a forbidden thing has not contaminated. For He said – may He be praised and exalted – 'Eat that which is good (*ṭayyib*) and do that which is proper' (Qurʾān, xxiii 53). Indeed, some commentators have held that what is meant by 'good' is 'lawful', but (the meaning of) the word 'good' is well known among men. He said – praised be He – 'Eat of that which we have provided to you, lawful, good' (Qurʾān, xvi 115, paraphrased), making a clear distinction between them, the lawful and the good.

Now, again; the pleasures of this world are divided into six classes. They are food, drink, clothing, sex, scent and sound. The most eminent and perfect of these is food; for food is the foundation of the body and the material of life. There is no way to enjoy anything else but with health, which it supports.

It is not forbidden to be meticulous about food, and to take an interest in it and specialize in it. He said – praised be He – 'Say: Who has made unlawful the adornment of God, which He brought forth for His servants, and the good things of sustenance?' (Qurʾān, vii 30). Whenever one of the companions of the prophet – God's blessing on him and his family – made a dish and was meticulous in it according to his state at that time, then he invited him; he (the prophet) responded to that (i.e., he did not disdain it). A certain philosopher has said, 'Four comprise the best things and complete (God's) grace: strong faith, blameless endeavour, wholesome food and salutary drink'. Therefore it is shown that there is no blame in taking pleasure in food and specializing in it.

I have come across a number of books composed on the making of dishes, which mention strange and unfamiliar things and include disapproved ingredients. When they are brought together, the soul is not reassured by them. Men disagree in their choice among the pleasures we have mentioned, some of them preferring food over the rest and some preferring others, such as clothing, drink, sex and sound. I am one who prefers the pleasure of food over all the other pleasures, so I composed this book for myself, and for whoever may want to use it in the making of dishes. In it I mentioned what I preferred, perhaps leaving out some obvious and well-known dishes in the interests of brevity. I have followed those with relishes, condiments, pickles, fish, *jūdhābs* and sweets that I have also preferred. I have aimed at brevity and succinctness rather than prolixity and longwindedness, and I pray God to give me aid and grant me success.

I have ordered it into ten chapters. This is their introduction:

Chapter One, *ḥawāmiḍ* (sour dishes) and their kinds

Chapter Two, *sawādhij* (simple dishes) according to their variety

Chapter Three, on *qalāyā* and *nawāshif* (fried and sauceless dishes) and their kinds

Chapter Four, *harāʾis* (porridges with shredded meat), *tannūriyyāt* (porridges with chopped meat) and dishes that resemble them

Chapter Five, *muṭajjanāt* (fries), *bawārid* (cold dishes), *maqlūba* (egg dishes), *sanbūsaj* (samosa) and things that serve the same function

Chapter Six, fish, fresh and salted

Chapter Seven, *mukhallalāt* (pickles), *ṣibāgh* (relishes) and *muṭayyibāt* (condiments)

Chapter Eight, *jawādhīb* (puddings served with roast meat), *akhbisa* (puddings thickened with flour or crumbs) and their varieties

Chapter Nine, *ḥalāwā* (sweetmeats) and their varieties

Chapter Ten, *qaṭāyif* (crepes), *khushkanānaj* (cookies, sweet biscuits) and things that serve the same function.

INTRODUCTION WHICH NEEDS TO BE KNOWN

[Wise men have said,] the cook must be knowledgeable, well versed in the principles of the dishes and proficient in making them. Let him take care to trim his fingernails lest he injure them [and ulcerate them], and not to let them grow long, lest dirt collect under them. Of pots, he will prefer [choose] the soapstone, then the earthenware, and in case of necessity, tinned copper. The worst (of food) is what is cooked in a copper pot that has lost its tinning.

Of wood, he will choose the dry and whatever does not have obvious smoke [because of its dampness], such as olive, [dry] oak, [oleander[1] and the trees that are for sale], and the woods that resemble them. He will avoid fig wood, because it produces much smoke, and whatever has dampness in it. He will know how much wood (to use).

He will choose *al-darānī* salt.[2] If none is available, then clean [white] salt free of dust and small rocks; [the best kind is that which has been dissolved and thickened (i.e. clarified)].

What is to be borne in mind about spices: Of coriander, that which is fresh, green in colour, dry. Of cumin and caraway and the like. Of cinnamon, that which is rough, thick, tightly coiled, with a penetrating aroma, burning to the tongue. Of mastic, that which has large, [white] lustrous grains, not pounded, free of dust

1. *Diflā* (oleander) may be an error for *dafnī*, Greek *daphnē*, bay laurel; oleander wood is poisonous.
2. That is, rock salt mined in Andarān, near Nishapur, rather than sea salt.

and dirt. Of pepper, what is fresh, not old. [Of ginger, that which is *maghrūs*, 'implanted'.] He will clean all the spices extremely well and grind them fine.

Likewise he will wash the vessels and pots that have been used in cooking and beat them with brick dust, then with potash and pounded dry rose (petals). [He will perfume bowls with mastic and galangal, then scoop in them.] And he will wipe the pot, after washing it, with fresh citron [and orange] leaves.

He will choose a stone mortar for pounding meat; he will grind spices fine on a stone or pound in a copper mortar. In short, let him scrupulously pound the spices well and make them smooth, and wash the pots and utensils as much possible.

He will use much spice in *sawādhij* and even more in *qalāyā* and *nawāshif*, whether sweet or sour, and he will use little in *ḥawāmid* that have sauces.

The basic rule in all dishes is, when the pot is boiled, to be scrupulous in removing the scum and froth and dirt of the meat, and whatever might float on the surface of the pot along with the rising bubbles. Before that, wash the meat [in hot water and salt] to remove any blood and dirt that might remain in it, and clean it of any glands, [tendons and membranes].

The meat in *sawādhij* and *qalāyā* is stewed in grease [and a little sesame oil] before boiling. [It is the basic principle for eliminating the scum.] Dishes should be left until they settle on a quiet fire [one] good while (*sāʿatan jayyidatan* [*wāḥidatan*]) before ladling. So know that.

CHAPTER I

ON SOUR DISHES AND THEIR VARIETIES

AMONG the sour dishes are those sweetened with sugar, syrup, honey or date molasses, and those not sweetened or, properly speaking, sour; but everyone has decided that they should be in one chapter.

Al-Sikbāj.[1] The way to make it is to cut up fat meat medium and put it in the pot with water to cover it, [a bunch of] green coriander, a stick of cinnamon and the necessary amount of salt. Then, when it boils, remove its scum and froth with a spoon and throw it away. Then put dry coriander on it and remove the green coriander. Then take white onions, Syrian leeks and carrots, if in season, or eggplant (if they are not), and skin them all. Quarter the eggplant lengthwise and half boil it in salt water in another pot, then dry it and leave them in the pot on top of the meat. [Throw the spices on it and adjust its salt in it.] When it is nearly done, take wine vinegar and date molasses – some people prefer to use honey, but date molasses is more appropriate – and mix them, balancing the sweetness and sourness. Then pour them into the pot and boil it for a while. When the fire needs to be cut, take some of the broth and mix it with the necessary amount of saffron. Pour it into the pot. Then take peeled sweet almonds which have been split in half and leave them on top of the pot, with a few jujubes,

1. Middle Persian *sik* 'vinegar' and *bāg* 'stew'.

raisins and dry figs. [And put them on top of the pot.] Cover it awhile to grow quiet on the heat of the fire. Wipe the sides of the pot with a clean cloth and sprinkle rose-water on top. When it grows quiet on the fire, take it up.

Ibrāhīmiyya.[1] The way to make it is to cut up meat medium and put it in the pot with water to cover and the necessary amount of salt. Boil it so that it stews. Put in it a piece of strong linen, tied with pounded coriander, ginger, pepper and finely pounded [galingale] inside it. Then put pieces of cinnamon and mastic on it, and chop up two or three small onions finely and throw them in it. [Pound lean meat and make into meatballs according to the rule, and put them in.] When the ingredients are done, remove that cloth that the spices are in. You make a sauce with the juice of aged mild[2] sour grapes; if there is none, with fresh sour grapes squeezed by hand, without boiling, then strained, [or with filtered vinegar]. Beat sweet almonds, which have been finely pounded to a liquid consistency with water. Pour the sour grape juice on it and sweeten it a little with white sugar; let it not be strongly sour. (Sc. add it to the pot.) Leave it on the fire awhile to grow quiet, and wipe the sides with a clean cloth. Then sprinkle the top of it with a little rose-water, and when it is quiet, take it up.

Jurjāniyya.[3] The way to make it is to cut up meat medium and leave it in the pot, and put water to cover on it with a little salt. Cut onions into dainty pieces, and when the pot boils, put the onions on it, and dry coriander, pepper, ginger and cinnamon, all pounded fine. If you want, add peeled carrots from which the woody interior has been removed, chopped medium. Then stir it until the ingredients are done. When it is done, take seeds of[4] pomegranates and black raisins in equal proportion and

1. Presumably named for Ibrāhīm b. al-Mauṣilī, musician and arbiter of taste at the court of Harun al-Rashid.
2. *ᶜadhb*: pleasant, that is, not excessively sour.
3. From Gorgān, a city on the Caspian Sea.
4. 'sour; from the *Minhāj*'.

pound them fine, [macerate] well in water and strain through a fine sieve. Then throw them into the pot. Let there be a little bit of vinegar with it. Beat peeled sweet almonds pounded fine to liquid consistency with water, then throw them in the pot. When it boils and is nearly done, sweeten it with a little sugar, as much as needed. [That is, enough to make it pleasant, *yu*^{c}*adhdhibuhā*.] Throw [a handful of] jujubes on top of the pot and sprinkle a little rose-water on it. Then cover it until it grows quiet on the fire, and take it up.

Ḥummāḍiyya.[1] The way to make it is to cut up fat meat medium and leave it in the pot with water to cover and a little salt. Then bring it to the boil and throw the spices on it; and they are coriander, ginger, pepper and cloves, pounded fine and tied in a stout piece of linen. Throw in pieces of cinnamon. Then pound lean meat with spices and form it into meatballs, then put them into [the pot] after it has come to the boil. When they are done, remove the bag of spices. Take the pulp of large citrons, clean it of its seeds, and squeeze it well by hand. Then mix it with about a quarter as much sour grape juice and put it on the meat in the pot so that it boils awhile. Then take peeled sweet almonds, beaten to liquid consistency with water after being pounded fine, and add them to it. Then sweeten it with sugar; if you want, use syrup. Leave the pot on the fire to grow quiet. Sprinkle rose-water on top of the pot and wipe the sides of the pot with a clean cloth, then take it up.

Dīkabrīka.[2] The way to make it is to cut up meat medium and leave it in the pot. Throw on a little salt, a handful of peeled chickpeas, dry and fresh coriander and cut-up onions and leeks. Throw on water to cover and bring it to the boil, then take away its scum. Throw on wine vinegar and soy sauce, throw in a bit of

1. From *ḥummāḍ*, 'citron'.
2. From Middle Persian *deg bar ek*, 'pot on the embers'. The text indicates that the pronunciation had been Arabized to *dīkabrīka*.

finely ground pepper and cook it until its taste is evident. Some people sweeten it with a little sugar. When it is done, throw in some mixed spices, leave it to grow quiet on the fire, and take it up.

Zīrbāj.[1] The way to make it is to cut up fat meat small and put it in the pot, with enough water on it to cover it and pieces of cinnamon, peeled chickpeas and a little salt. When it boils, take away its scum. Then throw on a pound of wine vinegar, a quarter of a pound of sugar[2] and an ounce of peeled sweet almonds, pounded fine. Mix with rose-water and vinegar, then throw them on the meat. Throw on a *dirham* (each) of ground coriander, pepper and sieved mastic, then colour it with saffron.[3] Put a handful of split [peeled] almonds on top of the pot. Sprinkle a little rose-water on it, wipe its sides with a clean cloth, leave it on the fire to grow quiet, and take it up. If you like to put chicken in it, take a plucked hen and wash it and joint it. When the pot comes to the boil, throw it on the meat to become done.

Nīrbāj.[4] The way to make it is to cut up meat small or medium and throw it in the pot with a little salt and water to cover. Then boil it and take its scum away, and put chopped onions on it. If you like to put in carrots, put them. Throw on dry coriander, cinnamon, pepper, mastic, ginger and bunches of[5] mint. When it is done, take pomegranate seeds and a third as much of black [raisins]. Pound them fine, dissolve them in water, strain them and put them in the pot. Take walnuts and pound them fine, then milk them with water and throw them in the pot also. Put whole walnuts on top

1. First element unclear, from Persian *zīr* 'beneath; weak; anything dressed under roast meat'? Second element Middle Persian *bāg* 'stew'.
2. 'and if instead of sugar, some syrup, that is permitted; from the *Minhāj*'. (*Minhāj* actually reads 'Instead of syrup you could put a pound of pounded sugar crystals, that is permitted'.)
3. 'If you want it to be thick, put starch with the saffron; from the *Minhāj*'.
4. From Persian *anār* 'pomegranate' and *bāg* 'stew'.
5. Written above the line, in a later hand: 'fresh'.

of it. Take bunches of dried mint, then crumble them into the top of the pot. When the meat stews and the water decreases, sprinkle lean meat with spices and make it into meatballs (sc. and add them to the pot until they are done). Then sprinkle rose-water on the surface of the pot, rub its sides with a clean cloth and leave it on the fire to grow quiet, and take it up.

Ṭabāhaja.[1] The way to make it is to take sliced meat, cutting it up small. Take tail fat, slice it up and put it in the pot, with a little bit of water, half a *dirham* of pounded salt and a *dānaq* of saffron on it. When the tail fat melts and you have removed its cracklings, throw the meat into the pot on the fat. Throw on pieces of onion, bunches of mint and celery leaf, and stir it until its water dries up. Then throw on dry coriander, cumin, caraway, cinnamon and ginger, [all] finely pounded; set half the spices aside to throw on after it is done. Then take wine vinegar, sour grape juice and lemon juice and mix them, and throw some of all the spices on it. If you like to add some sumac juice, do so. Then moisten it with those liquids from time to time until it is completely done. Then take out the vegetables (*buqūl*), sprinkle aged soy sauce on it[2] and add the rest of the spices to it, with a little bit of pepper. Decorate its surface with egg yolks and sprinkle rose-water on it. Wipe the sides of the pot with a clean cloth, and leave it on the fire to grow quiet, and take it up.

Tuffāḥiyya.[3] The way to make it is to take fat meat, cut it into small elongated pieces and throw them in the pot, with a little salt and some dry coriander on them. Boil it until it is nearly done. Remove its scum and throw it away. Then cut onions small and throw them on top of it, with a stick of cinnamon, pepper, mastic, finely pounded ginger and bunches of mint. Then take sour apples, remove their pits and pound them in a stone mortar,

1. From Middle Persian *tābah* 'frying pan' and the diminutive suffix *-cha*.
2. 'and if there is none, sumac juice. From the *Minhāj*'.
3. From *tuffāḥ* 'apple'.

and squeeze out their juice and put it on the meat. Then beat some peeled almonds to a liquid consistency for it and throw them on it. Kindle the fire under it until it is done, and leave it on the fire to grow quiet. If you want to put a jointed hen in it, (do so), letting it cook until done, and you take it up.

Ḥiṣrimiyya.[1] The way to make it is to take fat meat, cut it up and throw it in the pot, with a little salt and dry coriander on it. Then cover it with water (sc. and boil), and take away its scum. Cut up onions (sc. and add.) Peel eggplant and half boil it in a separate pot with water and salt, then dry it and leave it in the (first) pot. Throw on bunches of mint and pieces of gourd with their peel and pulp (*shaḥm*) removed, and throw on pepper, mastic and finely pounded cinnamon. Then take fresh sour grapes, squeeze them well by hand and strain them in a fine strainer. Add a tenth as much lemon juice (to the sour grape juice) and put it in the pot. Then beat pounded peeled sweet almonds to a liquid consistency with a little water. Adjust its taste (i.e., the taste of the stew) with water and the desired amount of the almond milk. Then take a little bit of dry mint and crumble it into the top of the pot. Some people put some sourish apples on top of the pot, and it is good. Likewise, put in a jointed hen if you wish, after throwing the meat (in the pot). Then sprinkle the surface of the pot with rose-water, leave it on a quiet fire awhile so that it grows quiet, and take it up.

Ḥulwiyya, which is called *farḥāna*.[2] The way to make it is to cut up fat meat by itself, and tail fat by itself, and leave them in the pot with a little bit of salt, dry coriander and some chopped-up onions and carrots. Cover it with water and boil it until it is nearly done, and take its scum and throw it away. Then throw on pepper, ginger, mastic and finely pounded cinnamon. When is fully done,

1. From *ḥiṣrim* 'sour grapes'.
2. From *ḥulw* 'sweet' and *farḥān*, 'happy'; possibly from *faraḥ* 'happiness, wedding feast'.

take wine vinegar and sugar or syrup,[1] adjust its mixture according to desire and colour it with saffron (sc. and add to the pot). When it is nearly done, put split peeled sweet almonds, jujubes, peeled pistachios and hazelnuts, red raisins[2] and small pieces of sweet prunes on the surface of the pot. Sprinkle rose-water on the surface of the pot and wipe its sides with a clean cloth, and leave it on a quiet fire, and take it up. If you like, put a jointed hen with it after the meat is half boiled, to cook with it.

Rummāniyya.[3] The way to make it is to cut up fat meat medium and put it in the pot with a little spiced salt, and cover it with water (sc. and cook it) and thoroughly remove its scum. Then take eggplant and remove its black peel and quarter it lengthwise. Peel and quarter onions likewise, and peel gourds and clean them of their seeds and flesh, and cut them into strips. Throw all these in the pot, after half boiling them in a separate pot. Throw on coriander, cumin, cinnamon, pepper, mastic and bunches of mint, and cook until done. Then take sour pomegranates, strip them by hand and squeeze them well. Then strain (the juice) and throw it in the pot. Then crumble dry mint and put it on the surface of the pot. Pound a little bit of garlic and leave it in the pot also. You might put a jointed chicken in the pot to cook with the meat. Then leave it on the quiet fire awhile, then take it up.

Rībāsiyya.[4] It is meat boiled and (then) stewed with the spices. Throw on a little chopped onion, then squeeze rhubarb juice and throw it on. Beat some peeled, finely pounded sweet almonds to a liquid consistency and throw them in. Then leave it on the fire, its fire being quiet. Then leave it until it is done, then take it up.

1. 'or honey; from *Minhāj*'.
2. 'with their seeds removed: *Minhāj*'.
3. From *rummān* 'pomegranate'.
4. From *rībās* 'rhubarb (stem)'.

Summāqiyya.[1] The way to make it is to cut up fat meat medium, then leave it in the pot.[2] (Sc. Add water.) Then throw a little good salt on it. Then let it come to the boil until it is nearly done. Thoroughly take its scum away. Then throw on it boiled chard, cut in pieces a finger-width long, and carrots. Then take onions and Nabatean leeks, peel them, wash them in water and salt and put them on. If it is the season of eggplant, put it in with its black peel removed; boil it in a separate pot (i.e. before putting them with the meat). Then take sumac and put it in a separate pot, put a little salt and bread crumbs on it, boil it well and strain it. If you want, take a scalded, jointed hen and throw it in the pot. Pound lean meat fine and (sprinkle) the spices on it. Make it into medium-sized meatballs and throw them in the pot also. Put spices on it, namely dry coriander, cumin, pepper, ginger, cinnamon, finely mastic and bunches of fresh mint. Then take the mentioned sumac water and put it in the pot. Pound walnuts, beat them to a liquid consistency with water and throw them into the pot. Then crumble dry mint onto its surface, and throw in whole pieces of walnuts without pounding. Pound a little garlic, mix it with a little of the broth and throw it in the pot. Some people put whole raw eggs (sc. in the pot). Leave it on a quiet fire to grow quiet, then take it up.

[*'Amīrbārīsiyya*, which is *zirishkiyya*. It is made like *summāqiyya* except that it is with almonds. The best of it is made with fresh barberries.' *Minhāj*.] *Amīrbārīs* and *zirishk* are Persian names for barberry.

Līmūniyya.[3] The way to make it is to cut up meat and tail fat and leave them in the pot with a little salt, and cover them with

1. From *summāq* 'tanner's sumac', the tart dried fruits of which are used as a flavouring.
2. 'and stew it in sesame oil with onions', *Minhāj*.
3. From *līmūn*, 'lemon'. Arabic generally dislikes *ī* preceding a syllable that contains *ū*, and in modern Arabic this is often altered to *laimūn*. However, the text explicitly spells this name Līmūniyya.

water and boil until done. Take off its scum. Then take onions, leeks and carrots, if it is their season, or eggplant. Wash the onions and leeks with [warm] water and salt, and half boil [the eggplant] on its own in a separate pot, then leave them in the pot. If it is carrots, they do not need to be boiled separately. Then throw over it finely pounded dry coriander, mastic, pepper, cinnamon, finely pounded ginger and bunches of mint. Take a hen, joint it and put it in the pot, then throw the vegetables (*tawābil*) in it.[1] Take choicest[2] lemon juice, strain it from its sediment and its seeds, then throw it in the pot. Take peeled sweet almonds, pound them fine and beat to a liquid consistency with water, and leave them in the pot. Crumble bunches of dry mint into the pot, sprinkle it with rose-water and wipe the sides of the pot with a clean cloth. Then leave it on the fire to grow quiet, and take it up. Some people sweeten it with sugar. When it is eaten sweetened, omit the mint and eggplant.

Maghmūma, which is called *al-muqaṭṭaᶜa*.[3] The way to make it is to take fat meat and cut it up small, and cut tail fat in thin strips and cut them small. Take onions and eggplant, peel them and half boil them; they might not be boiled separately but peeled and cut into the pot of meat. Spread the tail fat in a layer on the bottom of the pot and a layer of meat on top of it. Sprinkle it with finely pounded spices, namely dry coriander, cumin, caraway, pepper, cinnamon, ginger and salt. Then spread a layer of eggplant and onions on the meat. Proceed according to this rule until they remain about four or five finger-widths from the pot (i.e., the ingredients stand four or five finger-widths high). Sprinkle the finely pounded spices on every layer as needed. Then

1. This instruction must be out of order, since it appears to mean that the chicken is added before the vegetables.
2. *sulāf*, a term that refers to wine made of the juice that which flows from ripe grapes without pressing. 'Free-run lemon juice' can scarcely be the exact sense here.
3. From *maghmūm* 'covered', *muqaṭṭaᶜ* 'chopped up'.

mix excellent vinegar with a bit of water and a little saffron, and put it in to cover the pot – and over that meat and the vegetables (*ḥawāyij*) by two or three finger-widths. Leave it to grow quiet on the fire, then take it up.

Mamqūriyya.[1] The way to make it is to cut up fat meat small and throw it in the pot, along with a little salt. Throw on water to cover, then bring it to the boil and remove its scum. When it is nearly done, throw on the spices coriander, cumin, cinnamon, mastic and pepper, and chopped onions. When it is done, throw on one part wine vinegar and two parts soy sauce. Throw a small handful of whole coriander seeds on the pot, sprinkle it with rose-water and leave it to grow quiet on the fire, and take it up.

Ḥubaishiyya.[2] The way to make it is to cut up fat meat medium, then throw it in the pot with a little salt and water to cover. Boil it and take off its scum. When it is nearly done, throw on chopped-up onions, which you have washed with warm water and salt, and peeled carrots from which you have removed that which is inside them (viz. the woody core). Throw on dry coriander, cumin, cinnamon, mastic and pepper. Then take the necessary amount of black raisins and pound them fine, then macerate them by hand and strain them. Take two parts of their juice and one part of good sharp vinegar, and throw them in the pot. Pound some walnuts and macerate them with the mentioned juice, and throw them on it. Crumble bunches of dried mint onto the pot. Leave the pot on the fire to grow quiet and take it up, after wiping its sides with a clean cloth.

Mishmishiyya.[3] Take fat meat, cut it up small and put it in the pot with a little salt and water to cover. Then boil it and take away its scum. Then cut up onions, wash them and throw them on the

1. From *maqara* 'to macerate (fish) in vinegar'.
2. From *ḥubaish*, 'the guinea-fowl', presumably because of its speckled plumage.
3. From *mishmish*, 'apricot'.

meat, and throw on the spices coriander, cumin, mastic, cinnamon, pepper and finely pounded ginger. Take dry apricots and soak them in hot water, then clean them and throw them into another pot. Bring them to a light boil, then take them down, macerate by hand and strain them through a strainer. Take the juice and make sauce (for) the pot with it. Then beat finely pounded sweet almonds to a liquid consistency with some of the apricot juice and throw it on it. Some people colour it with a little saffron. Then sprinkle a little rose-water on top of the pot, wipe its sides with a clean cloth, leave it to grow quiet on the fire and take it up.

Nāranjiyya.[1] The way to make it is to cut up fat meat medium and leave it in the pot [with water to cover] until it boils. When it boils, remove its scum and throw the necessary amount of salt on it. Cut up onions and leeks and wash them with water and salt. Scrape carrots, cut them four finger-widths long and throw them in the pot. Throw on cumin, dry coriander, sticks of cinnamon, pepper, ginger, finely pounded mastic and bunches of mint. Then pound lean meat finely with the spices and make it into medium-sized meatballs. Take oranges, peel them, take the [white] flesh from them and squeeze them; let him who squeezes them not be the one who peeled them.[2] Then strain (the juice) in a filter and throw it in the pot. Take safflower (seeds) which have been soaked in hot water for a while, then clean them and pound them well in a stone mortar; and if there is none, then (in) a copper (mortar). Milk their juice by hand, strain it and throw it in the pot. Then crumble bunches of dry mint on top of the pot, wipe its sides with a clean cloth and leave it on the fire until it settles, and take it up.

Nārsūn. This is a Persian name, and its origin is *anār sirk*, which means pomegranate and vinegar. The way to make this dish is to cut up fat meat medium, then throw it in the pot and cover

1. From *nāranj*, 'the (sour) Seville orange'.
2. Perhaps so that the dish will be flavoured with the juice alone, with none of the oils or bitterness from the peel.

it with water. Throw some salt on it and boil it, and remove its scum. When it is nearly done, throw on coriander, cumin, pepper, cinnamon and mastic, all finely ground except for the cinnamon; leave it as sticks. Cut up onions, wash them and throw them in the pot with bunches of mint. Put meatballs in the pot, made from lean meat pounded with the spices. Then take pomegranate seeds, pound them finely, mix them with wine vinegar, filter it and throw it into the pot. Take peeled walnuts, pound them fine, mix them with hot water and put them on the dish. Then adjust its flavour according to desire; let there be enough walnut for the stew to have a consistency. Then throw whole pieces of walnut on the pot and crumble bunches of dry mint into it. Sprinkle a little rose-water on it, wipe its sides with a clean cloth and leave it on the fire to grow quiet, and take it up.

Maṣūṣiyya.[1] The way to make it is to cut up fat meat medium and put it in the pot with water to cover and a little salt. When it boils, remove its scum. Throw on a bunch of celery (leaves), cut from their roots and stems and cleaned, and some chopped onions, and the spices coriander, cumin, pepper, mastic and sticks of cinnamon. Then throw on it enough good wine vinegar to cover it, and colour it with a little saffron, and throw whole raw eggs on it. Leave it on a quiet fire awhile, then take it up.

SECTION ON YOGURT AND WHAT IS COOKED FROM IT

Al-Maḍīra.[2] The way to make it is to cut up fat meat medium, then put it in the pot[3] with a little salt and water to cover, then boil it and remove its scum. When it is nearly done, take large

1. From *maṣṣa* 'to suck'. Originally a preparation of suckling kid; see Chapter V.
2. From *maḍara* 'to turn sour' (of milk).
3. 'with tail fat, and if there are pullets in it, joint them; *Minhāj*'.

onions and large Nabatean leeks also, peel them, cut off their tails, then wash them in water and salt, dry them and throw them in the pot. Throw on dry coriander, cumin, mastic and finely pounded cinnamon. And when it is done and its water has dried up and nothing remains but the fat, ladle it into a dish. Then take the necessary amount of Persian yogurt, throw it on the pot.[1] Leave it until it comes to the boil. Then reduce the heat from it and stir it. When its boiling subsides, return that meat [and the vegetables] to it. Cover the pot, wipe its sides and leave it to grow quiet on the fire, and take it up.

Buqūliyya.[2] The way to make it is to cut up fat meat medium and throw it in the pot with a little salt and water to cover. When it boils, take its scum away. When it is nearly done, take vegetable leeks, cut them small, pound fine in the mortar and throw them in the pot. Then take lean meat, pound it with the known spices and a little bit of those leeks, make it into meatballs and throw them in the pot. When its liquid has dried up, throw on coriander, cumin, finely pounded pepper and sticks of cinnamon. Then throw the necessary amount of Persian yogurt on it. Crumble bunches of dry mint into its top. Wipe the sides of the pot with a clean cloth, leave it to grow quiet on the fire and take it up.

Labaniyya.[3] The way to make it is to cut up meat and throw it in the pot with a little salt and water to cover [and boil it] until it is nearly done. When it stews in its fat and most of the water has dried up, throw chopped, washed onions and leeks on it, and eggplant, quartered lengthwise and half boiled in a separate pot; and afterward, dry coriander, pounded cumin, mastic, sticks of cinnamon and bunches of mint. Then boil it in the remainder of its liquid until it is completely done. Throw Persian yogurt on it in which you have put pounded garlic. Crumble bunches of dry mint

1. 'Put salted lemons and fresh mint in it; *Minhāj*'.
2. From (*kurrāth*) *al-baql* 'vegetable (leeks)'.
3. From *laban* 'milk, yogurt'.

into the top of the pot. Wipe the sides of the pot with a clean cloth, leave it on the fire to grow quiet for awhile, then take it up.

Buqūliyya [Mukarrara].[1] The way to make it is to cut fat meat medium and throw it in the pot with a little salt and water to cover. When it boils, take its scum away. When it is nearly done, throw the known spices on it. Then take green coriander [and bunches of mint], strip their leaves and throw them in the pot. Take vegetable leeks which have been cut small with the knife, then pound them in a stone mortar and throw them in the pot. Pound lean meat with the spices and mix a little of those pounded leeks with it, make it into meatballs and throw them in the pot. And when its liquid has dried up, (sc. throw into the pot) a little finely ground pepper, ginger and mastic. Then throw the necessary amount of Persian yogurt on it. Crumble bunches of dry mint into its top, wipe the sides of the pot with a clean cloth, leave it on the fire awhile to grow quiet, then take it up.

Mujazzaᶜa.[2] The way to make it is to cut fat meat medium, throw it in the pot with a little salt and cover it with water. When it boils, remove its scum. Cut up two or three onions and throw them on. Then take two or three bunches of chard for the pot of meat and wash them, after cutting them (in pieces) four finger-widths long, and throw them in the pot. Throw on dry coriander, cumin, mastic, cinnamon and pepper. When it is done, throw on Persian yogurt in which you have put a sufficient quantity of pounded garlic. Then when the pot grows quiet on the fire, sprinkle a little nigella on top of the pot. Wipe its sides and take it up.

ᶜUkaika.[3] The way to make it is to take fresh tail fat, cut it small and melt it, and take its cracklings out. Then take fat meat, cut it small and throw it on the melted fat, stirring until it is browned. Then put on enough water to cover (the meat) and a little

1. 'Repeated *Buqūliyya*'.
2. From *mujazzaᶜa* 'variegated'.
3. Apparently diminutive of *ᶜakka* 'magpie'; sense obscure.

salt, and leave it until it is done and it dries up (sc. and nothing is left) except for the fat. Throw on dry coriander and cumin, both finely pounded, and cinnamon, ground pepper and mastic. Then take a sufficient quantity of Persian yogurt, put pounded garlic in it, throw it on the pot and leave it until it boils. Then cut the fire under the pot and leave it [on] a quiet fire until the yogurt thickens. Throw away the fat on its surface. Then sprinkle a little finely ground cinnamon on it, wipe the sides of the pot with a clean cloth and take it up.

Maṣliyya.[1] The way to make it is to cut up fat meat and boil it as usual, and remove the scum. When it is done, throw on a handful of chopped onion, a little [salt,] ground dry coriander, cumin, pepper, sticks of cinnamon and mastic. When its liquid has dried up and the fat appears, take dried whey, pound it fine, throw hot water on it and macerate it well by hand until it becomes like sour yogurt (in appearance) and of the same consistency, then throw it in the pot. Grind a little garlic and throw it in the pot with bunches of fresh mint. Sprinkle some finely ground cinnamon on the surface. Then wipe the sides of the pot with a clean cloth, leave it on the fire awhile to grow quiet and take it up.

1. From *maṣl* 'dried whey'.

CHAPTER II

ON PLAIN DISHES ACCORDING TO [THEIR VARIETY]

Isfānākhiyya.[1] The way to make it is take fat meat and cut it up medium. Then cut fresh tail fat into strips, melt it and set its cracklings aside. Throw the meat in that fat and stir it until it is browned. Then put on enough separately heated water to cover (the meat) and throw in a little salt. Then boil it and remove its scum, and throw a handful of soaked peeled chickpeas on it. Take fresh spinach, wash it in water and cut up with a knife (into pieces) a finger-width long, after setting aside its lower roots. Pound it in a stone mortar and throw it in the pot. When it is nearly done, throw on [ground] dry coriander, cumin, pepper and mastic, slender sticks of cinnamon and a little finely pounded garlic. Then increase the water in the pot as needed, and let it (the water) be warm. When it has boiled awhile, throw the necessary amount of clean washed rice on it, and kindle the fire under it until it thickens and becomes smooth. Then leave it on a quiet fire awhile and take it up. Then you will have prepared finely pounded lean meat for it and made it into small meatballs. Throw them in the mentioned fat and spices. When you ladle the dish out, put the necessary amount of that fried meat and its fat on its surface. Also sprinkle finely pounded cinnamon on it, and use it.

[*Liftiyya* (turnip stew) is made with rice and turnips and meat.

1. From *isfānākh* 'spinach'.

Karanbiyya (cabbage stew) is made like *isfīdhabāj*, and cabbage is cut into it. *Qannabīṭiyya* (cauliflower stew): The best variety uses fresh white cauliflower. It might be cooked with various things. Let cauliflower be among its vegetables (*tawābil*). Usually it is cooked with rice. (*Minhāj*)]

Rukhāmiyya.[1] It is rice with milk, cooked until it becomes thickly congealed. Then you ladle it out and put meat on it which has been fried in tail fat and spices, (having been made) into meatballs, as mentioned in *isfānākhiyya*. Sprinkle cinnamon on it. You might make it another way, which is to boil the meat, and when it is done and little of its liquid remains, throw the necessary amount of milk on it. When it boils and comes to a full boil, throw on it as much washed rice as it will bear. [And throw sticks of cinnamon and mastic on it.] When it is done and smoothly thickened, ladle it out and put the fried meat and cinnamon which we mentioned on its surface.

Āruzz Mufalfal.[2] The way to make it is to take fat meat and cut it up medium. Melt fresh tail fat and throw away its cracklings, then throw the meat on it and stir until it is browned. Sprinkle a little salt and finely ground dry coriander on it. Then leave water to cover on it and boil it until it is done, and throw its scum away. Remove it from the pot after its liquid has dried up and it has started to stew, lest it be dry. Throw on as much dry coriander, cumin, cinnamon and finely ground mastic as it will bear, and likewise as much salt. When it is completely done, take it up from the pot, having been dried of moisture and fat. Sprinkle a little of those mentioned spices on it. Then take a measure of rice and three measures [and a half] of water. Melt fresh tail fat weighing one third as much as the meat. Throw the water in the pot. When

1. From *rukhām* 'marble'.
2. From *āruzz* 'rice' and *mufalfal* 'made to resemble peppercorns, viz. cooked as separate grains'; there might also be influence from the Persian word *pulau* 'pilaf'.

it comes to [a boil], throw the melted fat on it. Throw mastic and sticks of cinnamon in it, then boil it until it comes to a full boil. Wash rice several times and colour it with saffron and throw it in the water; do not stir it. Then cover the pot awhile until the rice boils up[1] and the water is boiling. Then open it and arrange that meat on top of the rice, and cover it with a cloth over the lid, and wrap it so that the air does not enter it. Then leave the pot until it grows quiet on a gentle fire for awhile, then take it up. Some people make it plain, not coloured with saffron.

Shūrbā.[2] The way to make it is to cut up fat meat medium. Then melt fresh tail fat, discard the cracklings from it, throw the meat in the fat and stir it until it browns. Then throw on warm water to cover, a little salt, a handful of peeled chickpeas, slender sticks of cinnamon and bunches of dry dill (leaves). When the meat is done, throw on dry coriander, ginger and finely ground pepper. Increase the water which is in the pot with warm water, and kindle the fire under it so that it comes to a full boil. Then take the dill from the pot. Take cleaned rice which has been washed several times and throw the necessary amount in the pot, and leave it on the fire until the rice is done. Then cut the fire from under it and sprinkle it with cumin and cinnamon, both finely ground. Wipe its sides with a clean cloth and leave it on the fire awhile, then take it up. Do not leave it until the rice has thickened strongly. If you want, put in some meatballs of pounded meat.

1. The text reads *yafūz*, 'is victorious', clearly an error. Celebi emended *yafūz* to *yafūr*, 'boils up', and Arberry rendered this as 'swells', which is what we would expect in a modern pilaf recipe. Perhaps the sense is that the rice reaches the surface, as it does when it absorbs most of the water; it clearly has done so in this passage.
2. From Middle Persian *shor* 'salty' and *bā(g)* 'stew'. The spelling shows that this word was borrowed after final -g was dropped in Persian during the 10th century. Earlier this dish had been known in Arabic as *al-māʾ wal-milh* 'water-and-salt'.

Mujaddara.[1] It is made like *āruzz mufalfal* except that you don't colour it with saffron, and you add half as much lentils as the rice. Follow the method mentioned for *āruzz mufalfal.*

Iṭriya.[2] The way to make it is to cut up fat meat medium, melt tail fat, remove its cracklings, throw the meat in the fat and stew it in it. Then throw on a little salt and a stick of cinnamon, then throw on enough warm water to cover it. Cut up two onions and throw them (in), before throwing the water (on), with peeled chickpeas, stalks of chard and two handfuls of cleaned washed rice. Then, when the meat is done, throw in finely pounded dry coriander, pepper and mastic. When it comes to a full boil, add a handful and a half of *iṭriya* noodles to the pot. Then, when the pot is done, sprinkle finely ground cumin and cinnamon on its surface, and wipe its sides with a clean cloth, and leave it to grow quiet on the fire, and take it up.

Rāshtā.[3] The way to make it is to cut fat meat medium and put it in the pot. Put on water to cover, a stick of cinnamon, a little salt, a handful of peeled chickpeas and half that much of lentils. Boil it until it is done. Then add more water and bring it to a full boil. Then throw (in) *rāshtā*, which is dough kneaded hard and rolled out thin, then cut into fine thongs four finger-widths long. Then kindle the fire under it until it has thickened smoothly. When it has grown quiet on a gentle fire awhile, take it up.

[It is made from strongly kneaded unleavened dough which is made like thongs and put in water and cooked with or without meat. From the *Minhāj*.]

1. From *mujaddara* 'pock-marked'.
2. From *iṭriya*, ultimately Greek *itrion/itria*, originally a thin fried flatbread, later a sort of noodle. Recipes never give instructions to make *iṭriya* and they always measure it by handfuls, so it was evidently a dry pasta, possibly sold ready-made in shops. Probably it resembled the Italian *orzo*, as the modern Egyptian *ṭreyya* does.
3. From Persian *rishta* 'string, noodle'.

ᶜAdasiyya.[1] The way to make it is to cut up meat and melt tail fat as usual, and put the meat in the fat and stew it until it browns. Then put on a little salt, cumin and ground dry coriander, and cover it with water. When it is nearly done, put in chard (stalks) which have been washed and cut up (in pieces) four finger-widths long. When the chard is done, add the necessary amount of water. Then boil it, and when it comes to a full boil, put in as much washed cleaned lentils as the water will bear. Then kindle the fire continuously under it until the lentils are done. When it is smoothly thickened and you know that it is done, take as much garlic as the pot will bear, pound it fine and throw it in. Stir it with the ladle, then leave it on a quiet fire awhile, and take it up. When you ladle it out, leave lemon juice on it.

Ḥinṭiyya.[2] The way to make it is to cut up fat meat medium, then stew it in melted tail fat according to the previous recipe. Then throw on a little salt, ground coriander and pieces of cinnamon. When it is nearly done, add water according to the amount of wheat, with a little dry dill (leaves). When it comes to a full boil, take the necessary amount of peeled wheat, bruise it a little in the mortar, wash it and throw it in the pot. Take the dill out and kindle the fire under it until it thickens smoothly. When it has grown quiet on the fire awhile, take it up and sprinkle finely pounded cumin and cinnamon on its surface. If you like, squeeze fresh lemons on it.

[It is cooked on a quiet fire and the surface of the pot is not skimmed until it has cooked to rags. From the *Minhāj*.]

Farīkiyya.[3] The way to make it is to stew fat meat, which has been cut up small, in melted fat. Then cover it with water and throw a little salt and a stick of cinnamon on it. When the meat is done, throw a bit of ground dry coriander on it, then add a little

1. From *ᶜadas* 'lentils'.
2. From *ḥinṭa* 'wheat'.
3. From *farīka* 'green wheat, rubbed (*tufrak*) from the ears'.

more water. Take the necessary amount of new wheat, rub it from its ears, clean it, add it to the pot and leave it until it thickens – thicker than *ḥinṭiyya.* When it grows quiet on the fire, take it down and ladle it out. Put finely pounded cumin and cinnamon and a little melted fresh tail fat on its surface, and eat it.

Muhallabiyya, which is called *al-bihaṭṭa*.[1] The way to make it is to boil fat meat after cutting it up medium and stewing it in melted fat in the usual way, as we have mentioned. When it is done, add water and leave it so that it boils awhile. Throw in the necessary amount of salt, dry coriander, mastic and a stick of cinnamon. When the meat is done, make sauce with warm water according to need and to the quantity of rice. When the water is boiling, take as much rice as the water will bear, wash it, (sc. put it in the pot), colour it with a little saffron and sweeten it with either syrup or sugar – adjust the sweetness according to desire. Leave it on the fire awhile to grow quiet, then take it up.

Isfīdhabāja.[2] The way to make it is to stew meat which has been cut up medium in the melted fat of fresh tail fat until it is browned. Then throw on the necessary quantity of salt, finely pounded dry coriander, cumin and pepper, pieces of onion, a handful of peeled chickpeas and stalks of dill. Cover it with water, throw a little salt on it and boil it until it is done. Remove the onions and add a little warm water. Then take one part almonds and peel them, pound them fine and milk them with water, and put them in the pot, and make it into sauce as desired with the almond milk. If you want, before throwing on the milked almonds, put in meatballs made from lean meat pounded with the known

1. Presumably named for al-Muhallab b. Abī Sufra, late seventh-century governor of Khorasan. The manuscript spells the second word *bihaṭṭa*, indicating a pronunciation even closer to the Punjabi *bhatt* (Urdu *bhāt*) than Arberry's reading, *bahaṭṭa*.
2. From Middle Persian *sped* 'white' and *bāg* 'stew'. The sense was a plain stew, with no sweet or sour flavouring and minimal spicing; most recipes did not contain almond milk.

spices and a scalded hen which has been washed and jointed. Then remove the dill and break whole eggs on its surface. Wipe the sides of the pot with a clean cloth and leave it on the fire to grow quiet, and take it up.

Sughdiyya.[1] The way to make it is to cut up fat meat and throw it in the pot, and (sc. throw) on it pieces of onion, two *dirhams* [of coriander, scraped sticks] of cinnamon and two *dirhams* of salt. Stir it continuously, and when it stews and its aroma spreads,[2] throw a handful of peeled chickpeas on it and stir it.[3] Then put on water to cover[4] and some[5] dill. When it boils, take the dill out of it. Then take finely pounded peeled almonds which have been beaten to a liquid consistency with water, and throw the whites of eggs on them and beat it well. Then throw it on the pot and adjust with enough salt for it. Then take light strips of meat which have been half boiled and seasoned[6] with salt. Arrange sticks crosswise on top of the pot, put those strips on them and fumigate them in the vapours that rise from the pot. When the pot is done, throw the strips of meat on top of it along with egg yolks which have been taken with their whites. Then take lean meat and pound it fine with the cleaver (sc., first on a cutting board) and then in the mortar, with the spices and the necessary amount of salt. Make it into meatballs and boil them with the strips of meat, and take them up and dip them in the egg whites; let them be hot so that the whites coat them and stick to them. Then put them in the pot with the strips. Wipe the sides of the pot with a clean cloth and cover it and leave it on the fire awhile to grow quiet. Then sprinkle cumin and finely ground cinnamon on its surface, and take it up.

1. From Sughd or Soghdia, seat of an ancient Persian kingdom.
2. 'That is, the aroma of the spices; *Minhāj*'.
3. 'Then, if you wish, throw a jointed hen or pullets on it; from the *Minhāj*'.
4. 'and a little sesame oil; from the *Minhāj*'.
5. 'washed; from the *Minhāj*'.
6. Or made fragrant, *tuṭayyab*, possibly with *milh mutayyab*.

Shūrbā Khaḍrā᾿.[1] The way to make it is to cut up fat meat medium and stew it in melted tail fat. When it is browned, put in the necessary amount of salt, finely ground dry coriander, pieces of cinnamon and a handful of peeled chickpeas. Cover it with water and kindle the fire under it, and when it boils, throw its froth away. Take two bunches of fresh vegetable leeks, cut them up small with the knife, then pound them in the mortar and throw them in the pot. Then take one part lean meat; pound it well with the spices, a handful of peeled chickpeas, washed rice and a bit of those pounded leeks, make it into meatballs and throw them in the pot. When everything is done, add the necessary amount of water to the pot. Then take a quarter as much rice as the water, wash it several times and throw it in the pot. Then boil it continuously until it is entirely done; it will be closer to lightness (in consistency). Then leave it on the fire until it grows quiet, and take it up.

Mā᾿ wa-Ḥimmaṣ.[2] The way to make it is to stew meat in the usual way, as has been described, and throw in salt, coriander, as much cumin (sc. as is desired), a stick of cinnamon, peeled chickpeas, dill and a chopped onion. Then cover it with water and kindle the fire until it is done and casts off its fat. Then it grows quiet on the fire [and you take it up].

[*Mā al-Ḥimmaṣ.* Whites of eggs, pounded coriander and sesame oil are boiled. Then washed chickpeas and water are thrown in. Its scum is removed, and it becomes done. If you want, throw in fresh milk, and if you want, throw in broad beans with the chickpeas. *Minhāj*.] *Minhāj* actually calls for the white part of onions, rather than whites of eggs.

Mā᾿ al-Bāqillā.[3] It is made like that, using peeled broad beans, which have been soaked and split in half, in place of the

1. See *Shūrbā* above; *khaḍra᾿*, feminine of *akhḍar* 'green'.
2. 'Water and chickpeas'.
3. 'Water of broad beans'.

chickpeas. When you ladle it out, put a little lemon juice on it, or finely pounded sumac from which the seeds have been cleaned.

Māsh.[1] Stew meat in the usual way. Take mung beans and clean them of their peels. Add a quarter as much rice to them and follow the procedure mentioned in the making of *āruzz mufalfal*.

[*Māshiyya*. The way to make it is to chop onions small and fry them in sesame oil with pounded coriander and a little Darānī salt. Throw mung beans in hot water and macerate them until their peels come loose. Clean them and then throw them on the sesame oil in the pot. Then throw on water and pounded peeled almonds which have been beaten to a liquid consistency, and boil it until it is done. From the *Minhāj*.]

Mulabbaqa.[2] The way to make it is like *āruzz mufalfal*, except that it should contain half rice and the other half (a mixture of) lentils, mung beans and peeled chickpeas. Follow the procedure mentioned for making *āruzz mufalfal*.

1. From *māsh* '*Phaseolus mungo*: mung beans, green gram'.
2. From *mullabaq* 'softened, refined'.

CHAPTER III

MENTIONING FRIED DISHES, DRY DISHES AND THEIR KINDS

SOME fried dishes have sourness in them, some have saltiness and some have sweetness. This chapter will then mention all of those.

Al-ᶜAnbariyya.[1] The way to make it is to cut up meat into strips and pound them with the cleaver (sc. on a chopping board), then pound them again finely in the mortar. Then boil sumac with water, salt and a piece of the crumb of *samīd* bread, then macerate it by hand. Press out its juice out and strain it, and boil the pounded meat in it. Take one part (of the meat; viz. without boiling) and make it into meatballs with the spices. When it (the boiled meat and meatballs) is done and has absorbed its moisture, dry it on a tray. Sprinkle it with the spices coriander, cumin, pepper, mastic and cinnamon, all pounded fine, with a little dry mint, and mix everything. Then melt fresh tail fat in a soapstone frying pan and throw away its cracklings. Take that meat and throw it in the frying pan to fry in the fat, and stir it continuously until it is done, lest it become dry and parched. Then garnish it with whole raw eggs and leave it until it becomes quiet on a gentle fire. Sprinkle a little rose-water on it, wipe the sides of the pan with a clean cloth, and take it up.

1. From *ᶜanbar* 'ambergris', which was used as a flavouring; with this recipe, the name appears merely fanciful.

Mishmishiyya.[1] The way to make it is to melt [tail] fat[2] and throw away its cracklings. Cut up fat meat small, then leave it on that melted tail fat and stir it until it browns. Then put on water to cover, a little salt and a stick of cinnamon. Then take lean meat, pound it fine and make it into meatballs shaped like apricots, with a peeled sweet almond in the middle of each of them. When the meat boils in the water and you have removed its scum, throw those meatballs (sc. in the pot). Throw on dry coriander, cumin, mastic, cinnamon and ginger, all pounded fine. When its liquid has dried up and the fat remains, sprinkle a little vinegar on it so that it will have a little sauce. Then pound sweet almonds finely, mix them with water and colour them with saffron. Throw them in the pot and adjust its flavour according to desire; some people sweeten it with a little sugar. Then sprinkle rose-water on the surface of the pot, wipe its sides with a clean cloth and leave it on the fire to grow quiet awhile, and take it up.

Safarjaliyya.[3] The way to make it is to cut up fat meat small in thin strips. Then melt fresh tail fat, throw its cracklings away and throw the meat in it. Throw on a *dirham* of salt, two *dirhams* of finely ground dry coriander, a stick of cinnamon and a bit of mastic. Then put on water to cover, and when it is nearly done, throw in red meat pounded with the spices as meatballs. When the meat is done in boiling, take big ripe sour quinces, then peel them, remove their seeds, cut them into middle-sized pieces and throw them on the meat, to cook with it until they are done. Also take one part of those quinces, pound it and squeeze out its juice well by hand in a stone mortar.[4] Then strain it and throw it in the pot. Sprinkle the amount of five *dirhams* of wine vinegar on it.

1. From *mishmish* 'apricot'.
2. The text has *al-duhn* (the fat), with *alya* (tail fat) written in the margin to bring the wording into line with other recipes.
3. From *safarjal* 'quince'.
4. Logically speaking, 'in a stone mortar' should appear before 'and squeeze out their juice'.

Take the amount of ten dirhams of sweet almonds, which have been pounded fine and beaten to a liquid consistency with water, and add them to it. Then colour it with a little saffron, sprinkle a little rose-water on the pot and wipe its sides with a clean cloth. Then leave it on a quiet fire awhile so that it grows quiet, and take it up.

Nāranjiyya.[1] The way to make it is to cut up fat meat small, then melt tail fat and throw the pieces of meat in the pot. Throw on one *dirham* of salt and (of) dry coriander and stir it until it browns. Then throw on water to cover, boil it and remove its scum. Throw on pepper, mastic, a stick of cinnamon and finely pounded ginger. Chop onions and peeled carrots small and throw them in the pot. Then pound lean meat fine, put in a bit of fresh tail fat and the mentioned spices and make it into meatballs the size of oranges. Then throw them in the pot, and when they are set firm, take egg yolks and beat them well [with a little saffron]. Then remove the meatballs while they are hot and immerse them in those egg yolks so that they coat them, then return them to the pot for awhile. Then take them out and return them to the mentioned egg yolks three times. When they are nearly done, take a small quantity of (sour) orange juice and lemon juice and sprinkle it on the meat which is in the pot. Then take ten *dirhams'* weight of peeled sweet almonds and beat it to a liquid consistency with water, and throw it in the pot. Rub bunches of dry mint over the pot, wipe its sides with a clean cloth and leave it on a quiet fire for awhile, to grow quiet. Sprinkle a little [rose-water] on it. [Take it up.]

1. From *nāranj* 'sour orange'.

Fākhitiyya.[1] The way to make it is to cut lean fat meat[2] in small strips and stew it in tail fat as described before. Then cover it with water until it boils, and take its scum away. Make finely pounded lean meat into middle-sized meatballs and put (spices) in them,[3] then throw them in the pot. Put in small pieces of onions and throw in a little salt, cumin, coriander, pepper, mastic and cinnamon, all ground fine. When it is nearly done, take Persian yogurt and strained sumac juice, mix them together and then throw them in the pot. Take peeled walnuts, pound them fine and beat them to a liquid consistency with the sumac juice. Throw them in the pot. Then crumble bunches of dry mint into the pot and leave it to grow quiet on the fire awhile. Then sprinkle a little rose-water on it, wipe its sides with a clean cloth and take it up.

Mudaqqaqāt Ḥāmiḍa.[4] The way to make it is to cut lean meat into thin strips, then pound them finely and throw in the spices, namely coriander, pepper, cinnamon and mastic, [and chickpeas and a little onion], then make it into meatballs which are smaller than oranges. Melt fresh tail fat, throw in the meatballs and stir them until they brown, then cover them with water. Chop two or three onions and throw them in the pot. When it is done and casts

1. From *fākhita*, 'the wood dove', because the purplish colour resembles its throat patch.
2. In every other recipe in this book, a distinction is made between fat meat, *laḥm samīn*, and 'red' meat, *laḥm aḥmar*, which is lean meat. Only in this recipe is meat described as fat and 'red' at the same time. This was a scribal error, or at least it was felt as such, to judge from the fact that the manuscripts derived from this book have chosen one description or the other. The London manuscript of *Kitāb al-Ṭabīkh* calls for *laḥm aḥmar*, and *Kitāb Waṣf al-Aṭᶜima al-Muᶜtāda* calls for *laḥm samīn*.
3. The word 'spices' has been omitted here, and as a result this passage might be read 'put them (the meatballs) in it (the pot), then throw them in the pot'. The London *Kitāb al-Ṭabīkh* repeats this absurd wording, but *Kitāb Waṣf* says to put spices in the meatballs, as described in all other meatball recipes, and then to put them in the pot.
4. 'Sour pounded (meat)'.

off its fat, sprinkle it with a little lemon juice or sour grape juice – or both of them mixed together – or sumac juice or pomegranate juice. Crumble bunches of dry mint onto the pot and throw in a little mastic, pepper and cinnamon. If you like, sprinkle a little wine vinegar on it and colour it with saffron. Then sprinkle the surface of the pot with a little rose-water, wipe its sides with a clean cloth, leave it on the fire awhile to grow quiet, and take it up.

Būrān.[1] The way to make it is to take eggplant and boil it lightly in water and salt, then take it out and let it dry awhile, then fry it in fresh sesame oil until it is done. Peel it and leave it in a plate (*ṣaḥn*) or large bowl (*qadaḥ*), and mix it well with a ladle until it becomes like a pudding. Throw in a little salt and dry coriander. Then take Persian yogurt, mix garlic with it, throw it on that eggplant and mix it well with it. Then take lean meat and beat it well [and make it into small meatballs], and take fresh tail fat (sc. and melt it), and throw the meatballs into it[2] and stir them until they are browned. Then cover them with water and boil them until the water dries up and they return to their fat (i.e. begin to fry in the fat). Put them on the surface of the eggplant, sprinkle with cumin and finely pounded cinnamon and use it.

Shīrāziyya.[3] The way to make it is to cut meat small and stew it in melted tail fat in the usual way, then cover it with water and boil it until it is done. When it is done, sprinkle it with cumin, coriander, cinnamon and salt. When its liquid has dried up and it casts off its fat, throw the necessary amount of *shīrāz* on it, stir it lightly and leave it to grow quiet on the fire. Sprinkle cumin and finely ground coriander on it, and take it up.

1. From Būrān, the wife of the caliph al-Mamun, whose wedding was the medieval byword for lavishness. Many dishes based on fried eggplant are named for her.
2. The text reads *yusharraḥ al-laḥm fīhi*, '(the) meat is sliced into it'. This must be a scribal error for *yuṭraḥ al-kubab fīhi*, 'the meatballs are thrown into it'.
3. From *shīrāz*, name of a thickened yogurt product.

SECTION ON PLAIN AND SWEET DISHES OF THIS CHAPTER

Among them are:

Būrāniyya.[1] The way to make it is cut fat meat small. Melt tail fat and remove its cracklings, then throw (the meat) on it, along with a little salt and pounded dry coriander. Then stew it until it browns and its aroma spreads. Throw on water to cover, green coriander leaves [and a stick of cinnamon]. When it boils, remove the scum from it. The liquid decreases from it. Throw on a small amount of halved onions, a *dirham* of salt and two *dirhams* (total) of dry coriander, cumin, cinnamon, pepper and mastic, all pounded fine. Then pound lean meat as mentioned before, and make it into [dainty] meatballs, and throw them in the pot. Take eggplant, cut off its calyxes and pierce it with a knife, then fry it in fresh sesame oil or melted fresh tail fat, along with whole onions. When the meat is done, leave a little soy sauce on it if you like, and colour it with a *dānaq* of saffron. Arrange the fried eggplant [and the onions] on the meat in the pot, and sprinkle it with dry coriander and finely pounded cinnamon, and sprinkle a little rose-water on it. Wipe its sides with a clean cloth, leave it on the fire awhile to grow quiet, and take it up.

Baṣaliyya.[2] The way to make it is to cut fat meat into small thin slices. Melt fresh tail fat and throw away its cracklings, and throw the meat on the fat and stir it until it browns. Put water to cover on it, along with a little salt, green coriander leaves and a stick of cinnamon, and boil it and throw its scum away. When the water decreases from it, take fresh white onions, peel them, quarter them lengthwise and throw them in the pot, after washing them with water and salt. Let there be half as much onions as meat. Throw on cumin, coriander, pepper, mastic and cinnamon, all pounded fine.

1. See *Būrān* above.
2. From *baṣal* 'onion'.

Some people colour it with a little saffron. If you want it made sour, throw about ten *dirhams* of lemon juice or vinegar (on it). Leave it to grow quiet on the fire awhile. Wipe its sides and take it up.

Raiḥāniyya.[1] The way to make it is to cut lean meat into thin slices and stew it in melted tail fat until it browns. Then put water to cover on it, and when it boils, throw away its scum. Then throw on a little salt, dry coriander, cumin, pepper, mastic and cinnamon, all finely ground. Pound lean meat with the (usual) spices, make it into dainty meatballs and throw them in the pot. Then take two bunches of fresh spinach and cut their roots off, then cut it small with a knife and pound it a little in a stone mortar, then throw it in the pot. When it is done and its water has dried up, throw in a little pounded peeled garlic with a little salt and cumin. Then stir it and leave it to grow quiet on the fire awhile. Sprinkle finely ground dry coriander and cinnamon on it [and take it up].

Nujūmiyya.[2] It is meat fried in its fat with the known spices. Add a handful of peeled chickpeas to it.[3] When it is done, arrange whole raw eggs on it, sprinkle the spices – finely ground cumin and cinnamon – on it, and leave it on the fire to grow quiet awhile, then take it up.

Narjisiyya.[4] The way to make it is to cut up fat meat small, melt fresh tail fat and throw the meat in the fat. Throw on a little salt and finely ground coriander and stir it. When it browns, throw on water to cover and a handful of peeled chickpeas, then bring it to the boil and throw away its scum. Then take fresh onions

1. Apparently from *raiḥān* 'sweet basil', perhaps because the dish is greenish.
2. From *nujūm* 'stars'.
3. Since the recipe does not state that the chickpeas are cooked, we should presume that water has been added to the fried meat, as in the other recipes.
4. From *narjis* 'poet's narcissus', because of a fancied resemblance to the flower.

and cut them up small with green coriander leaves and carrots which are hewn (*yunḥat*) until they are peeled; remove their wood from inside them and cut them up into thin small hewn (pieces). Pound lean meat [with the spices], make it into small meatballs and throw them in the pot. Then throw the cut-up carrots and onions (sc. and green coriander) after that, and stir it. Throw in the spices: two *dirhams* (total) of coriander, cumin, mastic and finely scraped cinnamon. If you like, sprinkle a little soy sauce on it. Then arrange whole raw eggs on its surface – I mean (on) the dish – and sprinkle finely ground cinnamon on it. Wipe the sides of the pot with a clean cloth, leave it on the fire to grow quiet awhile, and take it up.

Manbūsha.[1] The way to make it is to take lean meat, pound it fine and remove the tendons and cartilage from it. Then boil it in water with a little salt until half boiled, and dry it off. Then melt fresh tail fat, and throw that meat in the fat and stir it until it browns. Put water to cover on it, and throw in a little salt, dry coriander and green coriander leaves. Then take a handful of peeled split chickpeas and throw them on the meat. Kindle the fire under it until it is done, and the water dries up and it returns to its fat (i.e. begins to fry in it its fat). Throw cumin, [pepper], cinnamon and ground mastic in it. Arrange whole raw eggs on its surface and sprinkle finely ground cinnamon on it. Sprinkle a little rose-water on it, wipe the sides of the pot with a clean cloth and leave it on the fire to grow quiet awhile, then take it up.

Madfūna.[2] The way to make it is to cut up fat meat small, melt tail fat and stew it in it. Then cover it with water, and throw on a *dirham* of salt, a *dirham* of finely ground dry coriander and a stick of cinnamon. When it comes to the boil, take its scum and throw it away. Take lean meat, pound it fine and boil it in water and

1. From *manbūsh* 'disinterred'.
2. From *madfūn* 'buried'. This dish and the preceding recipe may have been linked in some way. Perhaps they were habitually served together.

salt. Throw on it a handful of coarsely pounded peeled chickpeas which have been soaked in water awhile. Then take large eggplant, cut off its calyxes and remove all that fills its interior, taking care not to pierce (the sides). Then stuff it with that meat (sc. and ground chickpeas), and put in the known spices. Then arrange (the eggplants) in the pot, after cutting up some onions for them, which you will have thrown into the pot before them. Then colour the broth of the pot with a little saffron and sprinkle a *dirham* of dry coriander and (of) finely ground cinnamon on it. Sprinkle the surface of the pot with a little rose-water, wipe its sides with a clean cloth, and leave it until it grows quiet on a gentle fire awhile. Then take it up.

Būrāniyyat al-Qar^{c}.[1] The way to make it is to cut up fat meat small, melt fresh tail fat and throw away its cracklings, and throw the meat in the fat and stew it until it browns. Then throw on warm water to cover, a *dirham* of salt, green coriander leaves and a stick of cinnamon. When it boils, remove its scum. Then take onions in proportion to the meat, wash them in warm salted water and throw it in the pot. Then take gourd, remove its flesh and seeds, cut it up small, remove its outer skin and throw it in the pot. Make lean meat, which has been pounded with the spices, into meatballs and throw them in the pot. Colour the sauce in the pot with saffron. Throw in the necessary amount of salt, cumin, dry coriander, pepper, mastic and ginger, all finely ground. Sprinkle the top of the pot with a little finely ground cinnamon. Sprinkle a little rose-water on it, wipe its sides with a clean cloth, leave it on a quiet fire awhile to grow quiet, and take it up. If you want it made sour, do not colour it with saffron, and sprinkle about ten *dirhams* of lemon juice on it.

Khuḍairiyya.[2] The way to make it is to cut fat meat into small pieces, melt tail fat, throw its crackling away and throw the meat

1. See *Būrān* above; *qar^{c}* 'gourd'.
2. From *khuḍair* 'little green one'.

in the fat. Throw on a *dirham* of salt and (of) finely ground dry coriander and stew the meat until it browns. Then put on water to cover, thin sticks of cinnamon and green coriander leaves, boil it awhile, then throw its scum away. Take green broad beans, remove their husks and throw them in hot water for awhile, until their stickiness goes away. Wash them by hand and leave them awhile until they dry. Make finely pounded lean meat into dainty meatballs and throw them in the pot. Then throw the broad beans (into it) awhile later, and stir it. And when it is done, put on cumin, pepper, ginger and mastic, all finely ground, and stir. Then arrange whole raw eggs on the surface of the dish and sprinkle a little finely ground cinnamon on the surface of the pot, with a little rose-water. Wipe its sides with a clean cloth, leave it to become quiet on a gentle fire awhile, and take it up.

Rabīᶜiyya.[1] The way to make it is to cut up fat meat small, melt tail fat and stew the meat in the fat with a little salt and finely ground coriander. Then, when it is browned, put on water to cover, green coriander leaves and scraped thin sticks of cinnamon. When it boils, throw its scum away. Put on meatballs made from lean meat pounded fine with the spices, a handful of split soaked chickpeas, a handful of split peeled green broad beans and half a handful of jujubes, and stir. When it is done, put on the necessary amount of salt, cumin, pepper, mastic and ginger, all pounded fine, then arrange whole raw eggs on it. Sprinkle a little rose-water on the pot, sprinkle it with finely ground cinnamon weighing a *dirham* and leave it to grow quiet on the fire awhile, then take it up.

Makhfiyya.[2] The way to make it is to slice lean meat into strips four finger-widths long. Melt tail fat, throw its cracklings away and throw the meat in the fat. Throw on a *dirham* of salt and finely ground dry coriander, and stew it until it browns. Then

1. From *rabīᶜ* 'springtime'.
2. From *makhfiyya* 'concealed'. Spelled *mukhfiyya*, contaminated by the synonymous word *mukhfiya*.

add water to cover, green coriander leaves, sticks of cinnamon, [a handful of peeled chickpeas and a handful of onions chopped small]. When it boils, throw its scum away. Then pound lean meat fine and make meatballs from it with the spices. Then take boiled eggs and set their whites aside. Take the yolks and put them, remaining whole, in the middle of the meatballs. Throw them in the pot. When it is nearly done, throw on cumin, pepper, mastic and ginger, all pounded fine. Then take eggs and beat them well. Take those strips (of meat) out (of the pot) and dip them in it (the eggs) while they are hot, then return them to the pot. Do that two or three times [so that] it coats the strips like a shirt. Return them to the pot. When its water has dried up from it, sprinkle a *dirham* of finely ground cinnamon on it. Sprinkle a little rose-water on the surface of the pot, leave it to grow quiet on the fire awhile, and take it up.

Dīnāriyya.[1] The way to make it is to cut fat meat into small thin pieces, melt tail fat and throw the meat in the fat so that it stews. Then throw on a *dirham* of salt and finely pounded dry coriander. Then put on water to cover, a stick of cinnamon and green coriander leaves. When it boils, remove its scum. Throw in pieces of peeled onion. Then take lean meat, pound it fine with the spices, make cakes in the shape of *dīnārs* from it, and throw them in the pot. Take big carrots, scrape their skin off and cut them into *dīnārs*, and throw them in the pot. Then take boiled eggs and cut them also in the shape of *dīnārs* and throw them in the pot. When they have cut the eggs, some people fry them in sesame oil before throwing them into the pot. When it is done, throw on mastic, pepper and finely pounded cumin. Sprinkle it with ten *dirhams* of aged soy sauce, to which about three *dirhams* of vinegar has been added. Sprinkle half a *dirham* of cinnamon on it. Wipe the sides of the pot with a clean cloth, leave it to grow quiet on the fire awhile, and take it up.

1. From *dīnār* 'name of a gold coin'.

Ruṭabiyya.[1] The way to make it is to cut lean meat into thin, small, elongated pieces, then melt fresh tail fat, throw away its cracklings and throw the meat in the fat. Throw on half a *dirham* of salt and a similar quantity of finely ground dry coriander, and stir it until it browns. Then put on warm water to cover it, and when it boils, remove its scum. Then put on a handful of peeled almonds and pistachios, coarsely pounded. Colour it with a little saffron and throw on cumin, coriander, cinnamon and finely pounded mastic, about two and a half *dirhams* in all. Take the necessary amount of finely pounded lean meat and make it into long meatballs, with a peeled sweet almond in the centre of each. Put them in the pot. Then take sugar-candy or other *ruṭab* dates: the necessary amount, (being) drowned.[2] Remove pits from the bottom of the dates with a packing needle and replace them with a peeled sweet almond. When (the stew) is done and its water has dried up and it returns to (i.e., fries in) its fat, arrange those dates on it, and sprinkle it with about ten *dirhams* of sugar spiced with the weight of a *dānaq* of camphor. Sprinkle a little rose-water on it, wipe the sides of the pot with a clean cloth, leave it to grow quiet on the fire awhile, and take it up.

Mudaqqaqāt Sādhija.[3] The way to make it is to cut up the fat meat small and throw it in the pot. Then take lean meat, cut it into thin strips and pound it fine, along with a little tail fat, a handful of crushed peeled chickpeas and a handful of washed rice. Then throw water to cover on the meat which is in the pot, then bring it to the boil. Throw large meatballs which you have made from that pounded meat (sc. into the pot). When they stiffen, remove them from the pot, and the meat also. Melt fresh tail fat and take out its cracklings, then throw the meat and the meatballs in the pot

1. From *ruṭab* 'dates at the sweetest stage of ripeness' (related to *raṭb* 'moist').
2. Or 'being suitable for immersing in syrup'.
3. 'Plain pounded (meat)'.

and stir them in the fat until they brown. Throw on a little salt, and coriander, cumin, pepper and finely ground cinnamon, weighing two *dirhams* (in all), and cover it with water. Throw on a stick of cinnamon and a ring of dry dill (leaves). When it comes to the boil, discard the dill and throw on a handful of washed rice and half a handful of peeled chickpeas. When it is done, cut the fire from it and leave it on a quiet fire awhile to become quiet. Throw half a *dirham*'s weight of finely ground cinnamon on it, wipe the sides of the pot with a clean cloth, then take it up.

Khashkhāshiyya.[1] The way to make it is to cut lean meat into small slices. Melt fresh tail fat and throw them in it to stew. Sprinkle it with half a *dirham* of salt and a like quantity of ground dry coriander, then cover it with warm water. When it boils, remove its scum, then put in a finely scraped stick of cinnamon and a little finely pounded ginger. Then make sauce with a pound and a half of hot water, and throw a hundred and fifty *dirhams* of sugar or honey on it. When the sugar has dissolved, sprinkle a handful of poppy seed meal on it and stir it well until it is done and thickened. Then throw thirty *dirhams* of fresh poppy seeds on it,[2] and stir it until it is mixed. Then colour it with saffron, sprinkle a little rose-water on the surface of the pot, wipe its sides with a clean cloth, leave it to grow quiet on a gentle fire awhile, and take it up.

[And when it is ladled out, the nut oil (*duhn*) of *fālūdhaj* is put on it. *Minhāj*.]

ᶜUnnābiyya.[3] The way to make it is to slice lean meat into small thin pieces, melt fresh tail fat and remove its cracklings, and throw the meat in the fat so that it stews. Throw on half a *dirham* of salt and a like amount of finely ground dry coriander,

1. From *khashkhāsh* 'poppy'.
2. 'and if it is impractical, then dry poppy seeds pounded after boiling. *Minhāj*'.
3. From *ᶜunnāb* 'the jujube fruit'.

then cover it with warm water. Then take lean meat and pound it fine, clean it of tendons and gristle and throw a little of the known spices on it. Then make it into meatballs the size of jujubes, with a peeled pistachio inside each one. Then throw them into the pot. Then, when it is half boiled, dissolve saffron in rose-water thickly.[1] Take those meatballs out and put them in it, and when they are coloured, return them to the pot. When it is nearly done, sprinkle it with a *dirham* of cinnamon and finely ground ginger. Sprinkle ten *dirhams* of good vinegar on it, and scatter fifty *dirhams* of sugar on it. Then throw on a handful of fresh jujubes and half a handful of peeled sweet almonds, and colour it with saffron. Sprinkle a little rose-water on the surface of the pot, wipe its sides with a clean cloth, and leave it to grow quiet on the fire awhile, and take it up.

Fālūdhajiyya.[2] The way to make it is to cut lean meat in small elongated pieces, then melt tail fat and throw it in it, and stew it with a quantity of salt weighing a *dirham*, along with (sc. a like quantity of) dry coriander. Put water to cover on it and a piece of cinnamon,[3] and cook it until it is done and (only) the meat remains, browned, not parched. Then throw on the necessary amount of pounded sugar and honey and colour it with saffron. Put a handful of peeled sweet almonds in it. Then stir it continuously until it thickens, and leave it to grow quiet on the fire awhile.[4] Arrange fried white *sanbūsaj* on it, stuffed with almonds and sugar. Wipe its sides with a clean cloth, then take it up.

1. The meaning seems to be that you use so much saffron that the mixture is thick. The saffron water must indeed be strong, because it is being used to colour the meatballs so that they resemble jujubes.
2. From *fālūdhaj* 'a sweet based on ground almonds'.
3. 'the two mixed: *Minhāj*'.
4. 'If you want it to be very thick, throw an ounce or less of starch, macerated in water, on two pounds of sugar or honey, and it will thicken. When it is ladled out, it is garnished with white *sanbūsaj mukallal*. From the *Minhāj*'.

Bunduqiyya.[1] The way to make it is to slice lean meat into small pieces, melt tail fat and throw the lean meat in the fat. Throw on half a *dirham* of salt and a like amount of finely ground dry coriander and stir it until it stews, then put on hot water to cover. Throw on green coriander leaves and a handful of crushed peeled chickpeas. Then take a handful of boiled chickpeas and crush it in the mortar. Pound lean meat fine with the spices and make meatballs from it, with some of those ground chickpeas in the middle of each one; make them into meatballs resembling hazelnuts. Throw them in the pot, and when it is nearly done, throw on an amount of coriander, cumin, pepper and finely ground cinnamon weighing two *dirhams* (sc. in all). Then separate the yolks of eggs from their whites and arrange them on the surface of the pot. Sprinkle a little rose-water on it, wipe its sides with a clean cloth, leave it to grow quiet on the fire awhile, and take it up.

Muqarraṣa.[2] The way to make it is to take lean meat and cut it into strips, then pound it fine with the known spices [and a little garlic]. Melt fresh tail and throw away its cracklings. Make that meat into cakes and throw them in the fat until they brown. Then leave water to cover on them, and when it boils and they are done, and the water dries away from them and they return to their fat (i.e. begin to fry in their fat), sprinkle it with a little cumin, coriander and finely pounded cinnamon. Then leave it to grow quiet on the fire awhile, and take it up.

Fustuqiyya.[3] The way to make it is to take the breasts of chickens and [half] boil them in water and a little salt. Then dry them off and take the meat from upon the bones, and pluck it into fibres like threads. Return it to the pot and pour water to cover on it. Then take the necessary amount of peeled pistachios and crush

1. From *bunduq* 'hazelnuts'.
2. From *muqarraṣ* 'made into cakes (*qurṣa*)'.
3. From *fustuq* 'pistachio'.

them in the mortar and throw them in the pot. Stir it, then bring it to the boil. When it is done, throw on an amount of sugar weighing twice as much as the pistachios, then stir it until it thickens, and take it up.

Kurdiyya.[1] The way to make it is to take a suckling lamb which has been scalded (of its fleece) and washed clean. Then cut it into joints and boil it in water with a little salt and a stick of cinnamon. And then take from the pot and dry it off. Then take a quantity of fresh sesame oil and leave it in a pan of soapstone or tinned copper. When the sesame oil boils, throw on a ladle of the water in which the lamb was boiled.[2] Then take that meat and remove it from the bones and shred it,[3] then leave it in the pan and stir it continuously so until it stews. Then sprinkle it with dry coriander, cumin, pepper and finely ground cinnamon. Leave it with its top covered on a quiet fire to grow quiet awhile, and take it up.

Qaliyyat al-Shiwā.[4] The way to make it is to take cold roasted meat from last night and cut it up small. Take fresh sesame oil and throw it in the pan to boil, then throw the roasted meat on it and stir it. When its fat melts, throw on coriander, cumin and finely ground cinnamon. If you want it made sour, sprinkle it with a little vinegar coloured with saffron and arrange whole raw eggs on its surface. If you prefer, put lemon juice instead of the vinegar and do not leave the eggs on it. Leave it on the fire when it is gentle awhile, until it grows quiet, then take it up.

1. Apparently from *kurdī* 'Kurdish'.
2. This dangerous-sounding instruction is missing in *Waṣf*.
3. *yushazzā*, literally 'splinter it'.
4. 'Fried dish of roast meat'.

SECTION

As for dishes of chicken, when (the chicken) has been boiled, joint it and stew it in fresh sesame oil with dry coriander, mastic and cinnamon.

If it is one of the sour dishes (*ḥawāmiḍ*), after the stewing, make a sauce with sumac water (viz. to make *summāqiyya*), or pomegranate seeds (*rummāniyya*); or lemon juice (*līmūniyya*) or sour grape juice (*ḥiṣrimiyya*), or both of them compounded; or in *zīrbāj*, (use) vinegar and sugar. Then pound peeled sweet almonds fine and beat them to a liquid consistency with water and throw them in the pot. Sprinkle rose-water on it and crumble bunches of dry mint on its surface – except for *zīrbāj*, for mint is not left in it.

If it is *maṣūṣ*, stew it in sesame oil after boiling it, and throw on celery leaves and vinegar coloured with saffron. Some people put whole raw eggs on it.

If it is *mamqūr*, after the stewing, throw on two equal parts vinegar and soy sauce [with a little bit of the boiling water].

If it is *muṭajjan*, throw in a little bit of the boiling water and a bit of aged soy sauce, and when it is taken from the fire, squeeze fresh lemon juice on it. Before that, you will have fried it until brown in sesame oil.

If it is fried (chicken, (*dajāj*) *maqlū*), fry it in sesame oil and throw a little of the boiling water on it, and put whole raw eggs on it.

If it is *isfīdhabāj*, when the chicken is boiled with mastic, cinnamon and salt, pound sweet almonds fine and beat them to a liquid consistency with water. Throw them on it [with] a handful of soaked peeled chickpeas and a ring of dill, and put whole raw eggs on it.

If it is *khashkhāshiyya* or *fālūdhajiyya*, stew it in sesame oil.

Then throw[1] the boiling water onto it, and follow the procedure mentioned for making *fālūdhajiyya* or *khashkhāshiyya*.

If it is *ḥulwiyya*, stew it in sesame oil as we described. Then return its boiling water to it and throw the ingredients of *ḥulwiyya* on it, and follow the procedure explained in it.

Do not leave chicken dishes without dry coriander, and let there be no onion or garlic at all. This is the most important thing in making chicken dishes, so recognize that.[2]

1. Written over the line: *yuᶜād*, 'return'.
2. *fa-ᶜrif dhalika*; possibly *fa-ᶜzif* (sc. *ᶜan*) *dhālika*, 'so avoid that'.

CHAPTER IV

ON *HARĪSA*, *TANNŪRIYYA* AND OTHER DISHES MADE THAT WAY

Harīsa.[1] The way to make it is to take six pounds of fat meat, cut it up in elongated pieces and throw them in the pot [with water to cover]. Kindle the fire under it until it is nearly done. Then take (the meat) out, remove the meat from the bones, shred it (*yunashshal*) and return it to the pot. Take four pounds of good wheat which has been husked, washed and pounded, and throw it on. Then kindle the fire under it continuously from the beginning of night until the (first) quarter (of the night has passed), stirring it the whole time. Then leave it on a good fire, and throw jointed hens and sticks of cinnamon on it, and leave it until the middle of the night. Then beat it well until it becomes smoothly thickened.[2] Throw the necessary amount of salt on it. If it needs water, add hot water. Leave it until dawn, then beat it again, then take it up. Melt fresh tail fat and put it on its surface when you ladle it out. Throw finely ground cumin and cinnamon on it separately. Eat with aged soy sauce and fresh lemon juice.

Harīsat al-Āruzz, which is named *al-ᶜursiyya.*[3] The way to make it is to cut fat meat in elongated pieces, and make it like wheat *harīsa* (viz. the above recipe), except that there will be

1. Name of the dish; from *harasa* 'to beat'.
2. 'and if it thickens too much, it is a fault. *Minhāj*'.
3. '*Harīsa* of rice'; from *ᶜurs* 'marriage feast'. Cf. *farhāna* above.

coarsely pounded rice in place of wheat.[1] When the meat is thrown in it, follow the procedure mentioned in wheat *harīsa*. When you ladle it out, put melted chicken fat on its surface and sprinkle sugar on it.

Tannūriyya.[2, 3] The way to make it is to take five pounds of meat and cut it up medium. Then wash it and throw it in the pot with water to cover, a little salt and a stick of cinnamon. Boil it, then throw its scum away and throw dry coriander on it. Take two pounds of cleaned, hulled wheat, finely pounded; wash it and throw it in the pot. Throw on bunches of dill, adjust its salt and cover the pot; fill it with water to the degree that four finger-widths (of water) remain (above the wheat). Put it in the tandoor until morning. Then take it up, and put a *thurda*[4] under it. Sprinkle cumin and finely ground cinnamon on it, and use it.

Kabīs.[5] The way to make it is to cut up fat meat medium, wash it and throw it in the pot, with a handful of chickpeas, a handful of hulled wheat, the necessary amount of salt, sticks of cinnamon, dry coriander, cumin, mastic and bunches of dill on it. Let there be plenty of water. Put the fore and hind legs (*atrāf*, extremities) of a lamb one year old [with] the meat. Put the pot in the tandoor from the beginning of night until morning, and take it up. Crumble a *thurda* under it, and sprinkle cumin and finely ground cinnamon on it, and use it.

Sukhtūr, which is called *kaibā*.[6] The way to make it is to cut up meat small. Take the small intestines of sheep and wash them with hot water and soap once, a second time with hot water and

1. 'Then cook the rice with much milk (*laban*), and when it is done, throw the shredded meat on it, and beat it until steam comes out. *Minhāj*'.
2. From *tannūr* 'tandoor, clay oven'.
3. 'The best kind is made from lamb and veal. *Minhāj*'.
4. Alternative form of *tharīda*, the Arabian dish of stewed meat mixed with bread. Here it evidently means a layer of crumbled bread.
5. From *kabasa* 'to cram, stuff, insert'.
6. From Persian *sukhtū* 'gut' and *gīpā*, 'sausage'.

citron leaves, and a third time with water and salt, until they are clean. Then paint them inside and out with saffron and rose-water. Then pound lean meat with the (usual) spices and make little meatballs from it, and throw them onto hot water until they stiffen. Then take them up and throw them on that cut-up meat. Then take [a quarter as much] rice as the meat, and a quarter as much (as that) of chickpeas. Wash them several times, then mix them with the mentioned meat and the necessary amount of salt, and throw cinnamon sticks which have been hewn thin[1] on it. Colour everything with saffron, and sprinkle it with dry coriander, cumin, mastic, pepper, cinnamon and finely ground ginger. Some people add jointed scalded chicken to that. Then take those intestines, cut them into medium pieces and stuff them with that meat. Join them and sew them with linen thread, or they make them with a pin of dry wood.[2] Arrange them in the pot. Cover it with water and salt and the mentioned spices, and also colour the water with a little saffron. Put in pieces of fat meat cut in thin strips, and increase the water after boiling as much as necessary. Then put it in the tandoor, and put the lid on it (i.e. on the pot) [from the beginning of night] until morning. Then take it up and use it. If you want to make it without gut, put that described meat, rice and chickpeas in a pot with a narrow top and leave it in the tandoor, the water being more than it (that is, higher than the surface of the ingredients) by four finger-widths. And when it comes to the boil, stir it, cover the top of the pot and leave it in the tandoor until morning, then take it up.

Ṭafshīl.[3] The way to make it is to cut fat meat into elongated pieces, then throw them in the pot and put on water to cover; then, when it boils, remove its scum. Take eggplant and remove its

1. *manhūtan nahtan raqīqan.*
2. The sense seems to be: Pinch the ends of the pieces together and sew them with thread, or skewer the ends with sticks to hold the gut together.
3. Name of uncertain origin.

black peel. Cut off half its stems, quarter it lengthwise and leave it in the pot. Cut up a little bit of onion and large Nabatean leeks. If it is not the season for eggplant, put instead peeled carrots which have been cut up in elongated pieces. Then throw on the necessary amount of fresh celery (leaves) and bunches of fresh mint. Add as much vinegar as there is water. Throw on mastic, coriander, cinnamon, pepper and ginger, all those finely ground except the cinnamon. Colour it with saffron, put it in the tandoor and cover the pot until morning. Then take it up.

Akāriᶜ.[1] Take the trotters from a year-old lamb, wash them clean and put them in the pot with three times enough water to cover them. Leave on them a handful of peeled chickpeas, the necessary amount of salt, mastic, dry coriander, finely pounded cumin and[2] pieces of cinnamon. Put the covered pot in the tandoor from the beginning of night until morning, then take it up and use it.

[The best (trotters) are from lambs and kids. The way to do them is to stew them with ground coriander, salt, whole cinnamon, sesame oil and hulled chickpeas. Throw on water to cover it by four finger-widths inclusive. Take its scum away, throw dill in it and remove its scum a second time. Put dough around (the rim of) the pot and fuel it continuously until it is done. Half the water will remain. Then open it, and you will see. Throw a handful of rice on its surface so it will be done when it (i.e. the dish) is completely done on the coals. *Minhāj*.]

ᶜAdas Tannūrī.[3] Cut up fat meat in elongated pieces and put them in the pot. Throw washed chard on it. Take lentils, clean them, wash them and put them in the pot, and fill it with water to the degree that four finger-widths remain from it (i.e., the water stands above the lentils by a height of four or five finger-widths).

1. 'Trotters'.
2. Written above the line: *ṣaḥīḥan*, 'whole'
3. 'Oven-baked lentils'.

Leave it in the tandoor, covered, until morning, and take it up. Throw coriander and cumin in it, and pound a bit of garlic and throw it in. Then sprinkle finely ground cinnamon on its surface. Eat it with fresh lemons, and if it is not their season, then with salted lemons.

[*ᶜAdasiyya Mizza* (sourish lentil stew). The way to make it is to cook peeled lentils in water until they fall apart. Throw half a pound of wine vinegar, a like amount of sugar crystals or honey, a little coriander, sesame oil and a little salt a quarter pound (*rubᶜ*) of it. It is done, and it is taken up. *Minhāj*.]

Sikbāj Tannūrī.[1] To make this, cut up meat, throw it in the pot and put the spices and the vegetables (*tawābil*) with it. Dissolve date molasses with vinegar (sc. and add it), and colour all that with saffron. Then adjust its salt, and lower it into the tandoor, with its lid on, from the beginning of night until morning. Then take it up.

1. 'Oven-baked *sikbāj*' (q.v.).

CHAPTER V

ON *MUṬAJJANĀ*, COLD DISHES, *MAQLŪBA*, SAMOSAS [AND WHAT IS ANALOGOUS TO THEM]

Muṭajjan.[1] Take a suckling kid and scald it, then wash it well and cut it into joints, then boil it in vinegar. Dry it after boiling, and fry it in fresh sesame oil. Throw on dry coriander, cumin and cinnamon, all finely ground. Then, when it has browned, take it out of the pan and put it in aged soy sauce. Sprinkle coriander and finely ground cinnamon on it, squeeze fresh lemons over it, and take it up.

Ṣifa ukhrā, nāshifa.[2] Boil a jointed kid in vinegar, fry it in sesame oil and sprinkle with cumin, coriander and finely ground cinnamon. If you like it plain, boil it in water (instead of vinegar), and fry it in sesame oil, and throw on the mentioned spices.

Maṣūṣ.[3] Take a suckling kid, scald it and cut it up into joints. Half boil it in water. Then refine[4] fresh sesame oil in the pot, and strip off celery leaves and throw them in the oil. When it stews, throw the kid in the pot, throw on enough good vinegar to cover and colour it with saffron. Leave it on the fire until it grows quiet and is completely done. Throw a little mastic on it and take it up.

1. From *ṭajjana* 'to fry', from *ṭajin* 'copper pan'.
2. 'Another recipe, dry' (viz. with no sauce).
3. From *maṣṣa* 'to suck', because made with a suckling kid.
4. *yukhla*ᶜ; i.e. by frying spices in it; see *badhinjān bi-laban* below.

Maqlūba.[1] Take lean meat and cut it into strips, then pound it with the cleaver, then transfer it to the mortar and pound it as fine as possible. Take fresh sumac (berries), boil them in water, then strain after macerating it well. Put in the pounded meat and boil it until it is done and has absorbed all the sumac water, the water covering it twice (i.e., by twice its depth). Then take it up from the pot, sprinkle lemon juice on it and spread it out to dry. Then sprinkle it with some of the finely pounded spices – dry coriander, cumin, pepper and cinnamon – and [crumble into it] bunches of dry mint. Take walnuts, pound them coarsely and add to it. Take eggs, break them, throw them on it and mix them well with it. Then fry it as cakes with fresh sesame oil in a thin iron or copper pan. When (one) surface of them is done, then turn over the other surface. Then it is done; take it up.

Sanbūsaj.[2] As for *sanbūsaj*, it is that you take the meat described in the making of *maqlūba* and cut up the thin bread[3] used for that and stuff it with the mentioned meat, after cutting it into strips. Make it triangular (i.e., fold it around the filling to make triangular samosas), then stick it together with a bit of dough and fry it in sesame oil, then take it up. As for that which is called *al-mukallal* (crowned, viz. glazed), it is that you stuff it with sugar and finely ground almonds kneaded with rose-water, or with *ḥalwā ṣābūniyya*, instead of meat, and fry it in sesame oil. Some people take it out of the sesame oil (and) put it in syrup, then they take it up from it and leave it in finely pounded sugar, spiced with musk and camphor, for him who wants it.

1. 'Turned over'.
2. Presumably Middle Persian **sambōsag*, from *se* 'three' (referring to the triangular shape) and **ambōs* 'bread with seeds in it'.
3. The 'bread' is a sheet of raw dough. Conceivably *sanbūsaj* might have been made with pieces of baked flatbread, glued together with raw dough as described, but all other medieval descriptions of it (including the quote from *Minhāj* which appears in the margin), not to mention samosa-making in the modern world, are more consistent with raw dough.

[The way to make it is to make *mudaqqaqa*, and make it sour with lemon juice. Stuff *sanbūsaj* flatbread with it and fry it. From the *Minhāj*.]

Maqlūbat al-Shiwā.[1] The way to make it is to take cold roast meat and pound it finely with the cleaver. Put the known spices and walnut meats on it, and follow the procedure mentioned for the making of *maqlūba*, also with eggs. If you want it made sour, sprinkle a little lemon juice on it.

Mufarraka.[2] Take chicken livers and gizzards, wash them, boil them in water with a little salt, then take them out and chop them small. Then mix them with the whites of eggs, put the necessary amount of the described spices on them, and fry them in a pan with sesame oil, stirring continuously. If you want it made sour, leave some filtered lemon juice on it. If you want it plain, do not leave lemon juice or eggs on it.

Bazmāward.[3] The way to make it is to take hot roast meat which has cooled off a little and cut it up. Put on mint leaves, a little wine vinegar, salted lemons and walnut meats, and sprinkle it with a bit of rose-water. Pound it finely with the cleaver, moistening it continually with vinegar until it is well absorbed. Take excellent pithy[4] *samīd* bread and remove its crumb. Then stuff it well with that roast meat and cut it up with the knife into medium elongated pieces. Take an earthenware tub, moisten it with water and dry it, and sprinkle rose-water on it. Then arrange fresh mint (in a layer) in it, and pack it (i.e. the *bazmāwards*) in it, one upon another. Then cover it them with mint also. Leave it awhile and use it. It is also eaten the next day, and it is good.

1. 'Overturned dish of roast meat'.
2. From *mufarrak* 'rubbed'.
3. From Middle Persian *bazm* 'banquet' and *āward* 'that which brings'.
4. *mulabbab*; that is, with lots of pith or crumb. The significance is that this is a thick oven bread, not a flatbread.

Baid Muṭajjan.[1] Take boiled eggs, peel them and fry in sesame oil. Then sprinkle coriander, cinnamon and finely ground cumin on them. Then take them out of the pan and put them in aged soy sauce, and sprinkle those (i.e. the well-known) spices on them. If there is no soy sauce, leave a little water, salt and cinnamon in the pan after the eggs are taken out, and when it boils, pour it onto the mentioned eggs. You might also make it according to another recipe, which is that they are fried as whole raw eggs, rather than being boiled. Throw some of those spices on them and sprinkle some soy sauce on them.

Baiḍ Maṣūṣ.[2] Take fresh sesame oil, throw it in the pot and bring it to the boil. Then put celery (leaves) on top of it. When they fry (*yuṭajjan*), sprinkle them with a little coriander, cumin, finely ground cinnamon and a little mastic. Then pour a sufficient amount of vinegar on it, colour it with a little saffron and when it is fully boiling, break eggs on it (leaving the yolks) whole. When they stiffen, take it up.

1. 'Fried eggs'.
2. 'Eggs seasoned *maṣūṣ*-style'.

CHAPTER VI

MENTIONING FISH AND WHAT IS MADE FROM THEM

FISH are either fresh or salted, and we shall mention the ones that are preferred.

SECTION ON FRESH FISH AND THEIR DISHES

Samak Mashwī.[1] Take fresh fish, scrape its skin well with a knife, then split its belly. Wash it well and dry it. Take sumac and pound it well and throw its seeds away. Take half as much dry thyme and pound it also, and a third as much finely pounded peeled garlic. Take half as much walnuts as everything (sc. the sumac, thyme and garlic) and pound it. Mix everything, sprinkle it with some coriander, cinnamon, cumin and finely ground mastic, knead it with fresh sesame oil, and adjust its salt. Daub the fish inside and out with sesame oil and saffron dissolved in rose-water, and stuff its interior with that described stuffing. Tie it up with strong linen thread, put it on an iron skewer and lower it into the tandoor on a quiet fire, not flaming. Cover its top (long) enough that it is known that it is done. Then take it up. It is eaten hot or cold.

Samak Maqlū.[2] Take fresh fish, split it, wash it well, then cut it into medium pieces. Pound garlic, thyme and the known spices

1. 'Roast fish'.
2. 'Fried fish'.

and stuff them[1] with it, then fold the piece around that stuffing. Colour it with saffron and fry it in fresh sesame oil. After it is done, take it out of the frying pan and put it in aged soy sauce. Some people make something stuffed with the stuffing of *samak mashwī*, as described above.

Samak Musakbaj.[2] Cut up fresh fish medium and fry it in sesame oil, and throw a small amount of whole dry coriander on it. Throw it in wine vinegar [which has been] coloured with saffron and in which there are celery leaves.

Samak Mamqūr.[3] Cut it up medium, wash it, colour it with saffron and fry it in sesame oil. Throw finely pounded mixed spices on it. Then put it in vinegar and soy sauce, there being twice as much soy sauce as vinegar.

Māliḥ Nāᶜim.[4] The way to make it is to take fresh *shabbūṭ*,[5] split it open and take out what is inside it. Then wash it well, dry it off and salt it well and much. Wrap it in a piece of *kasā*[6] and roll it up. Then put it in a room or hot place which no draught crosses for half a day – or less, or more; and let it be a summer day. The way to determine whether it is done is by feeling it with the finger; if its meat has become soft under the skin, take it out of the cloth, then wash it well. Dissolve saffron in rose-water and paint it all, inside and out. Then take cumin, coriander and finely pounded cinnamon along with mixed spices, make delicate slashes in it (the fish) and put some of that (the spices) in them, and sprinkle (them) inside it also. Then put it in a frying pan of tinned copper or soapstone and pour sesame oil to cover on it. Then leave it on a quiet fire in a tandoor, with its lid on. When it absorbs the sesame

1. The following instruction makes this sound as if the stuffing is accomplished by folding the pieces of fish around the mixture, not inserting it into them.
2. 'Fish made into *sikbāj*'.
3. From *maqara* 'to macerate in vinegar'.
4. 'Soft salted (sc. fish)'.
5. *Barbus grypus Heckel*, a large Iraqi carp.
6. Name of a coarse woollen fabric.

oil and dries up and browns, take it up. It is eaten hot (and) cold. It might be eaten with eggplant fried with *kāmakh rījāl*.

SECTION ON SALTED FISH AND ITS DISHES

Among them:

Samak Maqlū bi-Khall wa-Rahshī.[1] The way to make it is to take salted fish, wash it well, then dry it off and fry it in sesame oil. Throw a handful of whole dry coriander in the pan. Then take the necessary amount of good vinegar, put it on sesame paste and mix it by hand, moistening it little by little with the vinegar until it has the desired consistency in terms of thinness and thickness. If you like, put a little finely pounded mustard in it, and it might be made with other (flavourings) than that. Then take the salty fish from the pan hot and leave it in it (i.e. in the sesame sauce). Pour the sesame oil remaining in the pan on it along with the mentioned coriander. Sprinkle coriander, finely pounded cinnamon and walnut [meats] on it. It is eaten hot and cold.

Māliḥ bi-Laban.[2] Take salted fish, wash it and cut it as we have described. Fry it in sesame oil and take it out hot. Throw it in yogurt in which you have put pounded garlic and sprinkle it with cumin, coriander and finely pounded cinnamon. It is eaten hot and cold.

Māliḥ Maqlū Sādhij.[3] Fry it in sesame oil and sprinkle the mentioned spices on it, finely pounded.

Māliḥ Mukazbar.[4] After washing it, fry the salted fish in fresh sesame oil, along with coriander. Take it out hot and throw it in vinegar coloured with saffron.

1. 'Fried fish with vinegar and sesame paste' (*tahineh*).
2. 'Salted fish with yogurt'.
3. 'Plain fried salted fish'.
4. 'Salted fish spiced with coriander'.

Mālih bi-Khall wa-Khardal.[1] Fry it in sesame oil as described, and take it out of the pan and leave it in vinegar in which you have put finely pounded mustard seed and a little finely pounded coriander. Colour the vinegar with a little saffron.

SECTION ON *ṬARRĪKH*[2] AND WHAT IS MADE FROM IT

The recipe famous among the people is to fry it [in sesame oil] and break whole eggs on it. Among its varieties are:

Maqlūbat al-Ṭarrīkh.[3] Take *ṭarrīkh* and fry them in sesame oil, then take them out and put them in a dish until they get cold. Then cut their heads and tails off, remove their backbones and pick their bones and spines clean – pick them extremely well, as well as you can. Crumble and shred (*yushazzā*) their flesh, then sprinkle it with dry coriander, cumin, caraway and cinnamon. Break eggs and throw them on it, and mix it well. Then fry it in sesame oil in the *maqlūba* pan, as *maqlūba* is fried, until both sides of it are browned, and take it up.

Mufarraka.[4] It is to fry *ṭarrīkh* and clean them of the bones as we mentioned, sprinkle the spices on them, break eggs over them and fry them in sesame oil in a big pan. Keep stirring until it browns like *mufarraka*, which has been mentioned before.

Ṭarrīkh Maḥsī.[5] Fry *ṭarrīkh* in sesame oil, pick their bones clean as before and throw the spices on it (the meat). Then take good vinegar and mix it with sesame paste, as was done before in

1. 'Salted fish with vinegar and mustard'.
2. *Ṭarrīkh* (so vocalized in the text), from the Greek *tarikhos* 'dried': whole dried fish from Lake Van in Armenia.
3. 'Overturned dish of *ṭarrīkh*'.
4. See Mufarraka, Ch. V.
5. 'Puréed *ṭarrīkh*'. A modern reader expects this to be *mahshi* 'stuffed', but the text explicitly spells it this way. Presumably the name is derived from *hasw* or *hasā* 'sip, soup' because the dish has a semi-liquid consistency.

making the salted (fish; i.e. *samak maqlū bi-khall wa-rahshī*). Put sesame oil in the pan and return the *ṭarrīkh* to it. Throw a handful of whole coriander on it, then fry for a second time and throw it into the vinegar and sesame paste. Leave a little sesame oil in the pan, refine it (by frying spices in it) and pour it on it. If you like, put walnut meats and peeled sesame seeds on it.

CHAPTER VII

ON PICKLES, RELISHES AND CONDIMENTS

THERE are many kinds which are served among dishes, to cleanse their greasiness from the mouth, to improve the appetite, to aid the digestion of food and to make food palatable. We shall mention a preferred selection, briefly, as we have said.

SECTION ON VINEGAR PICKLES

Na^{c}na^{c} Mukhallal.[1] Take large-leaved fresh mint and clean the leaves from the stalks, then wash them and dry them in the shade. Sprinkle aromatic herbs on them. If you like, add celery leaves and peeled cloves of garlic. Put it in a clean glass jug, cover it with good vinegar and colour it with a little saffron. Leave it until the leaves absorb the sourness of the vinegar and its sharpness is cut; and use it.

Bādhinjān Mukhallal.[2] Take medium eggplants and cut off half their stems and their leaves. Then half boil them in water and salt, take them up and dry them off. Then quarter them lengthwise and stuff them with fresh celery leaves, a few bunches of mint and peeled cloves of garlic, and pack them one on another in a glass jug. Sprinkle a little of the herbs and finely ground mixed spices

1. 'Pickled mint'.
2. 'Pickled eggplant'.

on them, cover them with good vinegar and leave them until they are thoroughly mature, and use them.

Lift Mukhallal Muḥallā.[1] Take medium turnips and peel them, then cut them in small pieces. Then sprinkle a little salt on them, and afterward sprinkle them with some mixed spices and the herbs, and rub them well into those (turnips) with the hand. Then take the necessary amount of vinegar, and put two ounces of honey in every pound, and colour it with a little saffron. Put enough vinegar and honey on the turnips to cover them. Put them in a glass jug, and stopper its top until they mature, and use them. As for (the kind) that is not sweetened, cut them up and boil lightly in water and salt, and sprinkle a little mixed spices on them. Cover them with vinegar, and when they are mature, use them.

Bādhinjān Maḥsī.[2] The way to make it is to take eggplant, cut its stems and leaves off and boil it lightly in water and salt. Then take it out and dry it off, and cut it into small pieces. Sprinkle a little salt and some of the herbs and mixed spices on them. Then take good, well-pounded pomegranate seeds, macerate them in good vinegar, filter them and throw their dregs away. Put that vinegar on the mentioned eggplant and mix it with it. Then take walnuts and almonds and pound them [coarsely]. Put peeled sesame seeds with them and toast them.[3] Then put a little sesame oil in a copper *dist*. When it boils, put the almonds, walnuts and sesame in it and stir them. Then put them on that eggplant with the sesame oil, and put it in a glass jug, and put some finely ground mixed spices on it. Then use it after (some) days.

As for smooth cucumbers, ridged cucumbers, onions and other (vegetables) which you want to pickle, put them in vinegar alone until they soften and mature, and use them.

1. 'Sweetened pickled turnip'.
2. 'Puréed eggplant'. See *Ṭarrīkh Maḥsī* above.
3. *wa-yuḥammaṣ*; although the following sentence begins 'then', this verb seems to refer to the next instruction.

Bādhinjān bi-Laban.[1] Take medium eggplant, cut off its leaves and half its stems,[2] and half boil it[3] in water and salt. Then take it out, dry it well and throw it in yogurt and garlic. Refine fresh sesame oil with a bit of cumin and coriander and throw it on it. Sprinkle a bit of mixed spices and nigella on it, and use it.

Qarᶜ **bi-Laban.**[4] Take gourds, peel them, throw away their pith and seeds and cut them small. Then boil them in water and salt until they are done. Take them out of the water and dry them. When they are dry, put them in Persian yogurt with which well-pounded garlic has been mixed. Sprinkle nigella on it, and use it.

Silq bi-Laban.[5] Take chard with large ribs, cut off the edges of its leaves and cut it into pieces the length of a span. Wash it, then boil it in water and salt until it is done. Then dry it and put it in Persian yogurt and garlic, and sprinkle a little nigella on it, and use it.

Shīrāz bi-Buqūl.[6] It is a good relish which stimulates the appetite and benefits (the digestion).[7] The way to make it is to take mint, celery and vegetable leeks. Strip[8] the leaves of the celery and mint, cut everything small with the knife and pound it in the mortar. Then mix it well with *shīrāz*. Sprinkle it with a little salt, as much as necessary, and finely pounded mustard, and scatter

1. 'Eggplant in yogurt'.
2. It seems certain that the eggplant is cut up, or at least quartered, before being boiled and thrown in yogurt, like the gourd in the following recipe.
3. *niṣf salqa* ('half a boiling'). Over the line is written the word *jayyidan* ('well'), which would seem to contradict it.
4. 'Gourd in yogurt'.
5. 'Chard in yogurt'.
6. '*Shīrāz* with vegetables'.
7. *yumri*ʾ; possibly the sense is more general, that it benefits the eater.
8. In *Kitāb Waṣf*, the green part of the vegetable leeks is stripped as well.

coarsely pounded walnut meats on its surface, and use it. If there is no *shīrāz*, then renneted yogurt (*al-laban al-mās*) which has been strained from the water which is in it will be its substitute. A little sour yogurt is mixed with it, and it is used.

Isfānākh Muṭajjan.[1] Take spinach, cut off the bottom of its stems and wash it. Then boil it lightly in water and salt, and dry it. Then refine sesame oil, throw it (the spinach) in it (the oil), and stir it until it gives off its fragrance. Then pound a little garlic and put in it, and sprinkle cumin, dry coriander and finely pounded cinnamon on it, and take it up.

SECTION ON CONDIMENTS

Among them:

Kāmakh Rījāl.[2] Several kinds of it are made according to one principle; they differ according to the flavourings (*hawāyij*) that are left in them. The way to make it is first to take the shell of a large [dry] gourd,[3] from which you have cleaned all the pulp and seeds which are inside it, and soak it in water for two hours. Then dry it [well], and leave five pounds of sour yogurt, ten pounds of sweet milk and a pound and a half of finely ground salt in it, and stir it. Then cover its top and leave it in the hot sun for several days. The making of it starts in June (*Ḥuzairān*), at the beginning of the hot season. Then throw three pounds of sweet milk on it in the morning of every day, and stir it morning and evening. Whenever it decreases, add milk, until the beginning of August

1. 'Fried spinach'.
2. *Kāmakh* is the name of a class of condiments made by culturing milk with mould or (as here) the indigenous bacteria that give cheese its flavour. *Rījāl*, from the Persian *rījāl* or *rījār*, has had various meanings, such as 'electuary' (medicine that is licked) and preserved fruit (from which comes the modern Turkish word for fruit in syrup, *reçel*).
3. *ẓarf yaqṭīn kabīr* [*yābis*].

(*Āb*). Take mint leaves, nigella and peeled cloves of garlic and throw them in it, and stir it. Add sweet milk when it decreases, as usual, until the middle of September (*Ailūl*), and cover its top until the beginning of October (*Tishrīn*).[1] Then take it out of the sun until it congeals, and use it.

As for its varieties, one of them is the plain, into which no flavourings at all are put. One of them is another variety into which you put nigella and garlic. Dry red rose petals, cut from the stems, are put in another variety.

Zaitūn Mubakhkhar.[2] Take olives when they are ripe. If you like, take them green, and if you like, take them black; the green is [better] for smoking. Bruise them, put the necessary amount of salt on them and turn them over every day until their bitterness goes away. Then put them on a tray woven of sticks for a day and a night until the moisture which is in them dries up. Then pound peeled garlic and dry thyme finely, and take a *dirham* of it, and an olive pit, a piece of cotton dipped in sesame oil and a *dirham* of walnut meats, and leave them on a quiet fire. Put that on it.[3] Then put the woven tray holding the olives on a stove (*kānūn*) into which you have thrown this described incense (*bukhūr*). Close its door, and cover the olives with a cup or a bowl so that the smoke from it does not get out. Stir them several times so that the smoke moves around in them, and leave it for whole day. Then take it up and throw on sesame oil, coarsely pounded walnut meats, toasted peeled sesame, garlic and finely pounded thyme. Then mix all of that well, and leave it covered in a glass or greased pottery jug for days. Then use it.

1. Presumably Tishrīn I, rather than Tishrīn II, November.
2. 'Smoked (incensed) olives'.
3. In stew recipes, when ingredients are put 'on a quiet fire', they are always in a pan or pot. Here, what is being put 'on a quiet fire' is not going to be eaten; it is an 'incense', a source of aromatic smoke. So the garlic, thyme, olive pit, oiled cotton and walnuts are evidently placed directly on the embers inside a *kānūn* (fireplace, burner).

Khall wa-Khardal.[1] Take sweet almonds, peel them, pound them fine, then beat them to a liquid consistency with sharp vinegar until they are thin (of a thin consistency). Pound mustard fine and mix it with the desired amount of it (i.e. of the almonds and vinegar) along with some mixed spices, and use it.

Milḥ Muṭayyab.[2] Take big crystals of Andarani salt, put them in a new earthenware jar and seal its top. Then leave it in a hot tandoor for a whole day, and take it out. When it is cold, grind it fine. Then take coriander, sesame, nigella, hemp seeds, poppy seeds, cumin, fennel (seeds), asafoetida leaves and anise, and toast everything, and mix it with it. The salt might be coloured after grinding by putting it into water in which there is saffron for a day and a night; then dry it and grind it again. It might be coloured the same way with sumac juice or water of vermillion (*asrīqūn*). If you want it green, (dye it) with chard water.

Bāqillā bi-Khall.[3] Take green broad beans as soon as they are rough.[4] Remove their external husks, then boil them in water and salt until done, and dry them off. Sprinkle a little caraway and finely pounded cinnamon on them. Pour a bit of sesame oil on them. Put good vinegar to cover on them, and use them.

1. 'Vinegar and mustard'.
2. 'Spiced salt'.
3. 'Broad beans in vinegar'.
4. *ᶜindamā yakhshun*. When the seeds are firm, or when the seed pod has a coarse texture, or when they are large? *Kitāb Waṣf al-Aṭᶜima al-Muᶜtāda* says 'near the time of cutting'.

CHAPTER VIII

JŪDHĀBS, PUDDINGS AND WHAT IS ANALOGOUS TO THEM

Jūdhāb al-Khubz.[1] Take the crumb of leavened bread and soak it in water or fresh milk until it sours.[2] Put sugar and finely ground almonds over it and under it, colour it with saffron and leave it on the fire until it gives off the aroma of its doneness. Stir it, then take it up, and when it is ladled out, sprinkle it with finely ground spiced sugar.

Jūdhāb al-Qatayif.[3] Take fried crepes stuffed with almonds and sugar, arrange them in a *dist* between two thin flatbreads and put it under the chicken.[4] Between every two layers, put sugar and spiced, finely ground peeled almonds, like the stuffing of the crepes. Pour fresh sesame oil on it. If you want, put fresh milk on it and add sugar. When it is done and it gives off its aroma, take it up.[5]

1. 'Bread *jūdhāb*'.
2. 'until it grows (matures); *Minhāj*'.
3. 'Crepe *jūdhāb*'.
4. 'That is, a fat chicken is hung over it. *Minhāj*'.
5. 'Some people put walnuts and their oil instead of almonds and their oil. *Minhāj*'.

Jūdhāb Khubz al-Qaṭayif.[1] Take the necessary amount of *qaṭāyif* bread.[2] Sprinkle a little rose-water in the dist and spread the bread in layers, with almonds and sugar or finely pounded pistachios between every two layers. Sprinkle rose-water on it. When the bread has been used up in the *dist*, pour a little fresh sesame oil on it and cover it with syrup. Then hang fat chicken coloured with saffron over it, and when it is done, take it up. It might be made on small *qaṭāyif* stuffed according to this method.

Jūdhāb al-Khashkhāsh.[3] Take two pounds of refined sugar and make it into thin syrup. Then throw a quarter (pound)[4] of *samīd* and half a quarter of poppy seeds on it, and colour it with saffron and thicken it.[5] Some people put honey on it. When it thickens, put it between two thin flat breads and hang the saffron-dyed fat chicken over it.

Jūdhāb Khabīṣ al-Lauz.[6] Take almond pudding and make it according to this description.

[The way to make it is to take almond pudding (*khabīṣ al-lauz*) and put it between two thin flatbreads, with almond oil over it and under it, and hang the fat chicken over it. *Minhāj*.]

1. '*Jūdhāb* of *qaṭāyif* bread'.
2. This sounds like a term applied to ordinary crepes when they are used as ingredient in a dish. However, it might mean some particular kind of crepe, possibly a particularly large one.
3. 'Poppy-seed *jūdhāb*'.
4. *rub*ᶜ; London adds, by way of explanation, 'of a pound'. 'Half a quarter' is one eighth of a pound, or $1^1/_2$ (Troy) ounces.
5. 'That is, cook it on a medium fire until it is done. Some people add sugar, honey. *Minhāj*'. (*Minhāj* actually reads: 'Some people add a quarter pound and half a pound of honey to the sugar'.)
6. 'Almond pudding *jūdhāb*'.

Jūdhāb al-Tamr.[1] Take four pounds of dry dates and put them in a *dist* (sc. with water).[2] Kindle a fire under it until they are done. Then macerate them well by hand and strain them through a sieve, then return them to the *dist*. Throw on half a pound of sugar, a quarter of a pound of honey, half a *dirham* of saffron, a pound of crumbled bread crumb, a pound of sesame oil and a quarter of a pound of peeled walnuts. Stir it until it is nearly done, and arrange it between two thin flatbreads. You might garnish it with almonds, and then it is *ᶜaṣīdat al-tamr* (date pudding). It might be made without either sugar or honey.

Jūdhāb al-Ruṭab.[3] Take a copper *dist* and sprinkle a little rose-water in it. Then spread a thin flatbread in it and arrange a layer of newly harvested ripe *khāstuwī*[4] dates on it. Then sprinkle it with a layer of finely ground pistachio and almond meats and toasted poppy seeds. Then (arrange) dates and (sprinkle nuts) on them again[5] as we have mentioned, until half of the *dist* remains, the top layer being of almonds and pistachios. Then pour on half a pound of syrup and an ounce of rose-water into which half a *dirham* of saffron has been thrown. Cover it with a thin flatbread, and hang over it a fat chicken, which has been stuffed with sugar, almonds and pistachios kneaded with spiced rose-water and has been coloured with saffron inside and out. When it is entirely done, take it up.

Sifat jūdhāb ākhar.[6] Take the crumb of *samīd* bread and

1. 'Dry date *jūdhāb*'.
2. 'with ten pounds of water'. This marginal note appears to be in the hand of the scribe who has been inserting material from *Minhāj*, though it does not credit *Minhāj*. The issue is somewhat academic, because the whole recipe, very slightly modified, is from *Minhāj*.
3. '*Jūdhāb* of *ruṭab* dates'.
4. Name of the leading Iraqi date variety for eating at the prized *ruṭab* stage of ripeness, soft and syrupy.
5. *yuᶜād al-ruṭab wa-fauqahu*.
6. 'Recipe of another *jūdhāb*'.

crumble it well with the hand. Then put it in a tinned copper *dist*. Mix finely ground almonds and pistachios and a little toasted poppy seed with it, and pour on an ounce of rose-water which has been mixed with a third of a *dirham* of saffron. Throw on syrup to cover. If you want, throw on dissolved sugar, or honey.[1] Hang a fat chicken over it, stuffed as described before, until it is done. Take it out and use it.

The way to hang chicken over *jūdhāb* is to hang it in the tandoor and watch it. When its fat is about to run, throw the *jūdhāb* under it.

SECTION ON PUDDINGS

Ṣifat Khabīṣ.[2] Take half a pound of the pith of *samīd* bread, which has been rubbed like breadcrumbs (*fatīt*), and a quarter pound of sesame oil. Put the sesame oil in a tinned copper *dist* and boil it. Scatter the mentioned bread on it little by little, and stir it on a quiet fire. Then throw sifted pounded refined sugar on it and stir it. Leave it moist. Ladle it out and sprinkle sugar on it.[3]

Ṣifa ukhrā.[4] Take a pound of sesame oil. Throw half a pound of water and half a *dirham* of saffron[5] on it. Mix it with an ounce of rose-water and a pound of honey, both at once.[6] Boil it and

1. *maḥlūl*, 'dissolved' is written following the word 'honey', but it seems more likely that the sugar would be dissolved, not the honey; cf. the second *sifa ukhrā* below. If the correct reading is *sukkar maḥlūl* (dissolved sugar), it seems not to be quite the same thing as *jullāb* (syrup); perhaps *jullāb* contained rose-water, as suggested by the name (from the Persian for 'rose-water'), though medieval recipes give descriptions of rose-free *jullābs*.
2. 'Recipe of pudding'.
3. 'Some people put fresh milk in place of the sesame oil. *Minhāj*'.
4. 'Another recipe'.
5. 'and a quarter of a pound of *samīd* flour. *Minhāj*'.
6. *fī mauḍi*ᶜ *wāhid*, 'at one placing'.

stir it with a poker until the fat is released. If you want, throw in a handful of poppy seed and five *dirhams* of peeled pistachios. Ladle it out and put finely pounded sugar under it and over it.

Ṣifa ukhrā.[1] Take a pound of sesame oil and put a pound of toasted *samīd* flour on it. Boil it and stir it until it gives off its aroma. Then throw a third of a pound of dissolved sugar or honey or date molasses on it. Cook it on a quiet fire and stir it with the poker until it casts off its fat, and take it up. If it is (the variety called *khabīs*) *sukkarī*,[2] put pounded sugar spiced with camphor under it and over it.

Khabīṣ al-Lauz.[3] Take a pound of finely pounded peeled sweet almonds and three pounds of sugar. Put the sugar[4] in a *dist* and dissolve it with two ounces of rose-water (sc. over a fire). When it is dissolved and starts to thicken, throw the pounded[5] almonds on it and stir it until it is done. Ladle it out, and put finely pounded sugar under it and over it. It might be made with flour; put two ounces of flour on the pound of sugar,[6] and follow the mentioned procedure.

Khabīṣ al-Qarᶜ.[7] Peel the gourd, clean it of its seeds and boil it well. Then put it on a woven tray.[8] Grind it in a stone mortar and squeeze it out with the hand. Then throw sesame oil in the *dist* and boil it, and afterward throw flour. After that, throw the gourd with it, then moisten it with syrup until it thickens, and take it up.

1. 'Another recipe'.
2. Sugar pudding.
3. 'Almond pudding'.
4. 'sugar' is written over the line.
5. 'pounded' is written over the line.
6. 'when it is nearly done. *Minhāj*'. (The complete passage in *Minhāj* reads: 'It might be made with flour; put the pounded sugar and two ounces of pounded peeled almonds on a pound of flour, and throw it on it when nearly done'.)
7. 'Gourd pudding'.
8. 'until it dries; *Minhāj*'.

Khabīṣ al-Jazar.[1] Take carrots, peel them and boil them, and take their wood (woody core) from their interior. Cut them up small and grind them, and follow the procedure for *khabīṣ al-qar*^{c}.

1. 'Carrot pudding'.

CHAPTER IX

MENTIONING SWEETMEATS AND THEIR VARIETIES OF THAT (SORT)

Ḥalwā Yābisa.[1] The way to make it is to take sugar, dissolve it with water and boil it until it thickens. Then take it out of the *dist* and put on a smooth floor tile until its heat subsides. Then pound an iron peg with a smooth head (into the wall),[2] and throw (the candy) on it and stretch it with the hand unceasingly. Return it to the peg like that until it turns white. Then throw it on the tile and knead pistachios with it, and cut it into strips and triangles. If you want, colour it with saffron or cinnabar (*isrinj*). Some of it might be rolled[3] with peeled almonds, sesame seeds or poppy seeds.

[*Ḥalwā Yābisa Sukkariyya.* It has many varieties. It is that you take sugar and put a quarter (*niṣf*, 'half', is crossed out) of a pound of water on a *mann* (two pounds) of it. Dissolve it and put it on a quiet fire until it becomes thick. When you take some of it and put it in the mouth or in water, it will be chewy. If it does not become chewy, leave it (on the fire) a little more. Then take it up, throw it on a stone and knead it with clipped (*muqarraḍ*) crushed peeled almonds, about two ounces. Roll it out and leave

1. 'Dry sweetmeat'.
2. The words 'into the wall' are omitted in *Kitāb al-Ṭabīkh*, but they reappear in *Kitāb Waṣf* and *Kitāb al-Wuṣla*, making it clear that this iron peg serves as a post on which to stretch the candy.
3. Or kneaded; *yulatt*.

it to dry, and take it up. If you want to put some saffron in it, let it be before it comes down from the fire. You might pound almonds fine and mix them with it. *Minhāj*.]

Ṣābūniyya.[1] The way to make it is to dissolve sugar, then take it from the *dist* and put it in a vessel. Then throw sesame oil (into the *dist*), and when it boils, throw some of the syrup on it, with an ounce and a half of honey to every pound of sugar. Stir it, and when it is nearly thickened, dissolve starch, throw it on it and stir it. Then keep moistening it with the rest of the syrup until it thickens, then throw finely pounded peeled almonds on it. When it is completely done, ladle it into a plate, spread it out and sprinkle finely pounded spiced sugar on it.

Fustuqiyya.[2] It is made according to the method mentioned previously, except that you put pistachios in place of the almonds. Leave it on the fire for something over an hour (*faḍla sā*ᶜ*a*), then roll it out on a smooth floor tile. When it is cold, cut it up into triangles and sprinkle finely ground sugar on them. It is also called *al-muqarraḍa* (that which is clipped).

Makshūfa.[3] The way to make it is to take sugar, almonds or pistachios, honey and sesame oil in four equal parts. Pound the sugar and almonds and mix them together. Take enough saffron to colour it and add it with rose-water. Then throw the sesame oil in the *dist* so that it boils (*yaghlī*) and boils up (*yafūr*). Put the honey on it and stir it until its foam appears, and throw the sugar and almonds on the honey. Stir it continuously on a quiet fire until it is nearly thickened, and take it up.

Lauzīnaj.[4] Take a pound of sugar and grind it fine. Take a third of a pound of finely ground peeled almonds, mix them with the sugar and knead it with rose-water. Then take bread made thin

1. From *ṣābūn* 'soap', because of its waxy texture.
2. From *fustuq* 'pistachio'.
3. From *makshūf* 'uncovered'.
4. From Middle Persian *lauzēnag* 'marzipan' (a curious word in that it uses the Aramaic and not the Persian word for almond).

like *sanbūsaj* bread – the thinner, the better – and spread out a loaf of that bread and put the kneaded almonds and sugar on it. Then roll it up like a belt and cut it into small pieces, and arrange them (sc. in a bowl). Refine the necessary amount of fresh sesame oil and put it on them. Then cover them in syrup to which rose-water has been added. Sprinkle finely pounded pistachios on them.

Fālūdhaj.[1] Take a pound of sugar and a third of a pound of almonds and pound them fine together, then spice them with camphor. Take a third of a pound of sugar, dissolve it with half an ounce of rose-water on a quiet fire, then take it up. When it has cooled off, throw the pounded sugar and almonds on it and knead them with it. When it needs to be strengthened, add sugar and almonds. Then knead it hard and make *ausāṭ*,[2] melons, triangles and other shapes from it. Then arrange them in a dish or bowl and use them.

Mukaffan.[3] Take a pound of sugar and a third of a pound of almonds or pistachios and pound everything finely. Knead it hard with rose-water. Then throw an ounce of sesame oil in a *dist*, and dissolve [half] a pound of sugar and make it into syrup. When the sesame oil boils, throw a third of the syrup on it and stir it continuously. Then throw on an ounce of starch dissolved in water and stir it [unceasingly] until it thickens. Then throw it on a smooth tile until it grows cold. Roll it out (and cut it) into small square pieces the size of the palm. Then put some of that kneaded sugar and almonds on it, and roll it in the form of *ausāṭ*. Then sprinkle spiced sugar on it, and take it up.

1. From Middle Persian *pālūdag*, 'purified', name of this preparation.
2. In *Kitāb Waṣf*, *ausāṭ* are canapés made by putting a meat filling on a flatbread, rolling it up and cutting slices through it, much like Lauzīnaj above. Apparently this is the shape that is meant: a rolled-up sweetmeat (perhaps with a filling) cut into slices, jellyroll fashion. In *mukaffan*, below, *ausāṭ* are described as being rolled (*yulaff*).
3. From *kafan* 'shroud'.

Barad.[1] The way to make it is to take excellent *samīd* flour, knead it thinly and leave until it ferments. Then the set up the *dist* on the fire and put sesame oil in it. When it boils, scoop some of that dough in a plaited ladle and move it with a tremor over the oil, so that whenever a drop of the dough drips into the sesame oil, it hardens. As it is done, piece after piece, scoop it out with another plaited (ladle), so that the sesame oil dries from it. Take the necessary amount of sugar,[2] dissolve it with rose-water and put it on the fire until it boils and takes its (proper) consistency. Then take it down from the fire and beat it, while it is in the *dist*, until it turns white. Then throw the *barad* on it, and put it on a smooth greased tile and gather it together in the shape of the mould. Then cut it into pieces and use it.

Samak wa-Aqrāṣ.[3] Take a pound and a half of sugar and half a pound of peeled sweet almonds, pound them finely and spice them with a little musk. Take half a pound of good clean honey and put it in the *dist* [with an ounce of rose-water] until it boils. Throw its scum away. Then dissolve an ounce of starch in rose-water and put it on the honey, and stir it awhile until it appears to have taken its consistency. Then throw the pounded sugar and almonds on it and beat it well with the poker until it coagulates. Then take it down from on the fire and leave it on a smooth tile until it cools off. Then make it into fish and loaves in the carved wooden moulds which are made for that purpose. Arrange the fish in a plate and arrange the loaves around them. You might make it into chickens and lambs and other shapes, all with the mould according to what is desired. You might take peeled pistachios and put them on the surface of the mentioned loaves. If you want, colour the fish with a little saffron dissolved in rose-water.

1. 'Hail'.
2. 'Sugar' is crossed out and 'honey' is written above the line, but it is likely that 'sugar' is correct, because of the instruction to 'dissolve' it with rose-water.
3. 'Fish and cakes'.

CHAPTER X

ON MAKING *KHUSHKANĀNAJ*, *MUṬBAQ*, CREPES AND THINGS MIXED WITH FLOUR THAT ARE ANALOGOUS TO THOSE

Khushkanānaj.[1] It is that you take excellent *samīd* flour and put three ounces of sesame oil on every [pound], and knead it hard, well.[2] Leave it until it ferments, then it make it into long cakes, and into the middle of each put its quantity of pounded almonds and sugar kneaded with spiced rose-water.[3] Then gather them[4] as usual, bake them in the brick oven and take them up.

Muṭbaq.[5] Make a dough like *khushkanānaj* dough, except that you put four ounces of sesame oil on every pound of flour. When you have made it into cakes and sculptured bread (*khubza manqūshan*) with a wooden mould which has been made for this purpose, put the necessary amount of *halwā sādhija* – the kind without almonds and pistachios, with little sesame oil – in the middle of it, between every two cakes.

Urnīn wa-Khubz al-Abāzīr.[6] The way to make *urnīn* is to

1. From Middle Persian *hushk* 'dry' and *nān* 'bread'.
2. At this point *K. Waṣf* adds 'with a little water', which is indeed necessary for both the kneading and the later fermenting.
3. 'and let the almonds be half as much as the sugar. *Minhāj*'.
4. This instruction may be connected with shaping the biscuit with a mould.
5. 'Surrounded'.
6. *Urnīn*, name of unknown meaning and origin; *Khubz al-Abāzīr*, spice bread.

put three ounces of fresh sesame oil on a pound of flour (sc. with a little water). Then make it into cakes, and put finely pounded spiced almonds, pistachios and sugar in the middle of them. Gather them and stamp them; let there be a mould for them like a box. Bake them in the brick oven. Some people take the necessary amount of dates, remove their seeds, knead them with a little rose-water, sesame seed and toasted poppy seed and put it inside them. As for *khubz al-abāzīr*, it is that you put four ounces of sesame oil and half a *rub*ᶜ of peeled sesame seed on a pound of flour, and knead it well. Then bake it in the brick oven and take it up.

Aqrāṣ Mukallala.[1] The way to make it is to take the necessary quantity of excellent flour, knead it half way between thin and thick and leave it to ferment. Then take sugar and finely pounded pistachios, knead them with syrup, spice them and make (the mixture) into thin cakes. Cover them with that dough and bake them in the brick oven. Take half a pound of sugar and dissolve it with an ounce of rose-water, then grind half a pound of sugar and sprinkle it on the dissolved sugar, and stir it unceasingly (sc. over a fire) until it gets its consistency. Empty it out into a vessel, then dip those cakes into it, and it will congeal on them. Then sprinkle spiced finely pounded sugar on them, leave them to cool and use them.

Qaṭāyif.[2] There are several kinds. One of them is the stuffed, which is the kind that is baked in elongated shapes. Put finely pounded almonds and sugar in them, fold them around it and arrange them (on a plate). Throw sesame oil, syrup, rose-water and finely pounded pistachios on them. Another is the fried, which is the kind that is baked in (round) cakes. Knead finely pounded almonds and sugar with rose-water and put it in them. Then fold them (around the filling) and fry them in sesame oil. Take them out, dip them in syrup and take them up. And then there is the

1. 'Crowned (glazed) cakes'.
2. 'Crepes'.

plain, which is the kind that is put in a dish and sesame oil is poured on them, and then syrup, rose-water and finely pounded pistachios.

Aqrāṣ Mukarrara.[1] Take *samīd* flour, knead it thin and leave it until it ferments. Take a pound of sugar and a third of a pound of almonds, pound them [and knead them strongly with rose-water and syrup]. Make thin cakes from (the mixture), then coat them with that dough. Fry them in sesame oil, take them out and dip them in syrup. Dust them with pounded sugar, then return them to the syrup the same way three times. Then sprinkle spiced finely pounded sugar on them, and take them up.

Faṭāyir.[2] It is dough that you make thin, then fry it as cakes in sesame oil in a frying pan. Take it out, dip in syrup and sprinkle sugar on it.

Mubaḥthara.[3] Take the crumb of *samīd* bread and rub it well with the hands, then mix pounded toasted peeled almonds and pistachios with it. Sprinkle a little sugar on it. Refine sesame oil (by frying spices in it) and throw it on it; then, after that, cover it with hot syrup with rose-water, and take it up.

Luqam al-Qāḍī.[4] There should be strength in the dough of this variety. When it ferments, take pieces the size of hazelnuts and fry them in sesame oil. Then dip them in syrup and sprinkle finely pounded sugar on them.

Ruṭab Muᶜassal.[5] Take drowned[6] fresh-harvested *ruṭab* dates and spread them out in the shade and the air for a day. Take them and remove their pits, and put a peeled almond in place of every pit. Then take two pounds of honey for every ten pounds of dates, and boil it on the fire with two ounces of rose-water [and half a

1. 'Repeated cakes'.
2. 'Unleavened breads'.
3. From *mubaḥthar* 'scattered around'.
4. 'The judge's morsels'.
5. 'Honeyed *ruṭab* (fully ripe) dates'.
6. Or 'suitable for immersing in syrup', *gharīq*; see Ruṭabiyya above

dirham of saffron]. Then throw the dates in it and stir them for awhile. Then take them up until they are cold. When they are cold, sprinkle them with finely pounded sugar spiced with musk, camphor and spikenard. Put them in glass jugs, and sprinkle that spiced pounded sugar on the tops of them. Cover them and do not open until the season is cold and it enters the Kānūns (i.e. the months of Kānūn I and Kānūn II, December and January).

Ṣifat ᶜamal ruṭab fī ghair awānihi.[1] Take large crumbly-dry dates, the stalks of which have not been pulled out. Take a green watermelon and hollow out [its top] the size of the hand. Then take its flesh out, but not the juice. Leave the necessary amount of those dried dates in it and replace its top. Leave it for a day and a night, then take them out of it, and it will be as if they were fresh-picked ripe dates.

[*Ḥasā*. The way to make it is to boil two pounds of water and sprinkle it with twenty *dirhams* of *samīd* flour, five *dirhams* of starch, ten *dirhams* of sugar candy and an ounce of almond oil. It is done, and it is taken up. It might be made with fresh milk instead of water, without starch.] (Not credited, but from *Minhāj*.)

Ḥais.[2] Take excellent dried bread or biscuit (*kaᶜk*) and pound it well. Let there be a pound of it and three quarters of a pound of fresh (*āzādh*) or preserved (*maktūm*, 'concealed') dates – let their seeds have been removed – and three ounces of pounded almond and pistachio meats. Macerate everything well and strongly by hand. Then refine two ounces of sesame oil (by frying spices in them) and pour it on it. Knead it continuously until it is mixed. Make it into balls (*kubāb*) and dust them in finely pounded sugar. If you want, replace the sesame oil with clarified butter. This is good for travellers.

1. 'How to make *ruṭab* dates out of season'.
2. Name of this ancient Arabian dish; literally, 'mixture'.

Shawābīr.[1] Take a round frying pan with raised sides and throw two ounces of sesame oil in it. When it boils, throw three ounces of honey in it. Then take half a pound of [toasted] *samīd* flour and mix it with two ounces of finely pounded peeled almonds, pistachios and hazelnuts and two ounces of finely pounded sugar. Then sprinkle it on the honey and stir it until it thickens and gives off its aroma. If it needs to be thickened, add some of the mentioned flour. Then take it up until it is cold, and overturn it on a smooth tile and cut it into triangles (*shawābīr*), and dip them in syrup. Then sprinkle spiced finely pounded sugar on them, and take them up.

Ṣifat ᶜamal al-Kabūlā.[2] It is what is called *ᶜaṣīda* (pudding). Toast three pounds of *samīd* flour and take it up. Then set up the *dist* on the fire, and throw in three ounces of sesame oil and a half [and a quarter] (i.e., three quarters) of an ounce of whole cumin seeds. When it boils and gives off its smell, pour two pounds of water on it and boil it awhile. Then throw two ounces of washed rice on it, and when it boils and the rice is done, throw the flour on it; let its throwing be a sprinkling. Stir it continuously with the poker. When the flour is used up, moisten it with a little sesame oil, about an ounce. When it thickens and is entirely done, and it gives off its fragrance, take it from the fire. Grease vessels with sesame oil and ladle it (into them). Put the boiled sesame oil, finely pounded walnut and pistachio meats and toasted peeled sesame seeds on its surface. Afterward, put syrup and honey on it, and eat it. If you want, put clarified butter on it instead of almond oil.

COLOPHON

Kitāb al-Ṭabīkh is completed, praise be to God forever. Muḥammad b. al-Ḥasan b. Muḥammad b. al-Karīm, the scribe,

1. 'Triangles'.
2. Recipe for making *kabūlā*, a name of uncertain origin.

the Baghdādī, who is in need of the mercy of God – exalted be He – wrote it for himself in the last tenth of Dhū al-Ḥijja, year 623 of the Hegira, (December 20–21, 1226 AD). God alone suffices for us. O God, pray for our lord Muhammad the prophet, and his family and companions.

[A final recipe appears on the endpaper of the book, not part of a chapter and possibly written by a different scribe:]

Ṣifat ʿamal al-Murrī. Rotted barley (*fūdhaj*) and flour, of each five pounds. Knead it[1] (the flour; sc. with water) without leaven or salt, and bake it and dry it. Pound it and the rotted barley fine, and knead them (together) in a green tub with (sc. the necessary amount of water and) a third as much salt. Put it in the sun for forty days in the heat of summer. Knead it every day in the morning and the evening, and sprinkle water on it. When it turns black, put it in a jug and pour a like amount of water (i.e. ten pounds) on it. Leave it for two weeks, stirring it at the two ends of the day (i.e. morning and evening). When it begins to bubble, leave it until it settles. When it settles, strain it and return the dregs to the tub and leave them in the sun for two weeks. Let a like amount of water be on it. Then stir it at the two ends of the day. Then strain it onto the first *murrī*, and put cinnamon, saffron and aromatic herbs on it. *Fūdhaj* is wheat or barley flour which you knead dry with hot water, without leaven or salt, and make into cakes which you pierce in the middle. Wrap them in fig leaves and press them into a jug and leave it in the shade until they rot, then take them out and dry them.

1. The passage might be read to mean that the flour and rotted barley are kneaded together, but in fact the bread dough (as in other *murrī* recipes) is made from wheat flour alone; the rotted barley is added later after baking, when it and the bread are pounded.

APPENDIX I

AL-BAGHDĀDĪ'S MANUSCRIPT AND CHELEBI'S PUBLISHED TEXT COMPARED

Introduction

Chelebi omitted all of al-Baghdādī's marginal notes in the notes to the cook except: [white] (modifying 'salt'), [the best kind is that which has been dissolved and thickened], [in hot water and salt] and [tendons and membranes].

Chapter I

Jurjāniyya. Chelebi incorporated 'sour' from *Minhāj*, but rejected al-Baghdādī's [That is, enough to make it pleasant.]

Zīrbāj. Incorporated 'If you want it to be thick, put starch with the saffron' from *Minhāj*.

Tabāhaja. Chelebi incorporated 'and if there is none, sumac juice' from *Minhāj*.

Ḥulwiyya. Chelebi incorporated 'or honey' and 'with their seeds removed' from *Minhāj*.

Rummāniyya. Chelebi plausibly read *al-milḥ al-tayyib*, 'good salt', as *al-milḥ al-mutayyab*, 'spiced salt' (recipe in Chapter VII). Likewise in **Summāqiyya**, but there the text is very clearly *al-milḥ al-tayyib*.

Al-Maḍīra. Chelebi incorporated 'with tail fat, and if there are pullets in it, joint them' and 'Put salted lemons and fresh mint in it' from *Minhāj*.

Buqūliyya [**Mukarrara**]. Chelebi omitted this recipe.

Chapter II

Sughdiyya. Chelebi incorporated 'That is, the aroma of the spices', 'Then, if you wish, throw a jointed hen or pullets on it', 'and a little sesame oil' and 'washed', all from *Minhāj*.

Chapter III

Mishmishiyya: Chelebi omitted [some people sweeten it with a little sugar], giving the impression that the flavour of the pot is adjusted with almonds, rather than seasonings.

Fākhitiyya. In the passage about making meatballs where the word 'spices' is missing, Chelebi rejected 'then throw them', understandably considering it a scribal error.

Būrāniyya. Chelebi omitted [and the onions].

Narjisiyya. Chelebi omitted the aside 'I mean (on) the dish'.

Būrāniyyat al-Qar^{c}. Chelebi read *^{c}arham* (for *^{c}asharat dirham*, 'ten *dirhams*') as 'one *dirham*'. The London manuscript corrected this to the more plausible larger amount. In later recipes, Chelebi recognized *ham* (*him*) as abbreviations for *dirham* (*darāhim*). For instance, in Dīnāriyya, where he read *thalāthat (darā)him*, 'three *dirhams*', as did the scribe of the London manuscript. (To my eye, however, this could as easily be read *thalāthīn (dir)ham*, 'thirty *dirhams*'.)

Khuḍairiyya. Chelebi read *luzūjatuhu* 'their stickiness' as *raghwatuhu* 'their scum'.

Ruṭabiyya. Chelebi may have dropped the sign of the accusative in *gharīqan*; in al-Barudi's edition, the word has been changed to *^{c}udhaiq* 'a little cluster' and moved before the words *qadr al-hāja* 'the amount needed'.

Khashkhāshiyya. Chelebi incorporated 'and if it is impractical, then dry poppy seeds pounded after boiling' from *Minhāj*.

Fālūdhajiyya. Chelebi incorporated 'If you want it to be very thick, throw an ounce or less of starch, macerated in water, on two pounds of sugar or honey, and it will thicken' from *Minhāj* (but rejected the sentence 'When it is ladled out, it is garnished with white *sanbūsaj mukallal*').

Chapter IV

Harīsa. Chelebi incorporated 'and if it thickens too much, it is a fault' from *Minhāj*.

Tannūriyya. Chelebi incorporated 'The best kind is made from lamb and veal', from *Minhāj*. The published text has a misprint, *jamal* (camel) for *hamal* (lamb).

Sukhtūr. In the passage which I have translated 'Then take [a quarter as much] rice as the meat', the word *marratain*, 'twice as much', precedes the word 'rice', but a horizontal line is written over it. Chelebi chose to read 'twice' and ignored the word [a quarter] written in the margin, but the London MS evidently saw the horizontal line as an indication that 'twice' was an error and read 'a quarter'. 'A quarter' is surely correct; apart from making an absurdly starchy sausage, twice as much rice as meat would burst the flimsily sealed gut as it cooked. *K. Waṣf* has 'the necessary quantity of rice, a third as much as the meat'.

Ṭafshīl. Chelebi omitted the sentence 'Cut off half its stems, quarter it lengthwise and leave it in the pot'. Clearly Chelebi's eye had fallen upon the following sentence, which also begins 'Cut'.

Chapter V

Sifa ukhrā, nāshifa. Chelebi titled this Muṭajjan Nāshif, which is very likely how the dish was known, but the words do not occur in al-Baghadadi's text.

Sanbūsaj. Chelebi read *yuqlā* 'fry' (the *sanbūsaj* in sesame oil) as *yulqā* 'throw'.

Chapter VII

Bāqillā bi-Khall. Chelebi omitted the instruction 'Sprinkle a little caraway and finely pounded cinnamon on them'.

Chapter VIII

Jūdhāb al-Khubz. Chelebi incorporated the *Minhāj* instruction *hattā yarbū* 'until it grows (matures)' – without parentheses – and rejected al-Baghdādī's 'until it sours'.

Jūdhāb al-Qaṭāyif. Chelebi incorporated 'Some people put walnuts and their oil instead of almonds and their oil' from *Minhāj*.

Jūdhāb al-Khashkhāsh. Chelebi incorporated the second half of the note from *Minhāj*, rendering it: 'Some people add honey', without parentheses.

Jūdhāb al-Tamr. Chelebi incorporated 'with ten pounds of water' from *Minhāj*.

Sifat Khabīṣ. Chelebi incorporated 'Some people put fresh milk in place of the sesame oil' from *Minhāj*.

Sifa ukhrā (the first). Chelebi incorporated 'and a quarter of a pound of *samīd* flour' from *Minhāj*.

Khabiṣ al-Qar[c]. Chelebi incorporated 'until it dries' from *Minhāj*.

Chapter IX

Samak wa-Aqrās. In the instruction 'Then dissolve an ounce of starch', Chelebi seems to have unconsciously substituted *tudhāb* for the synonymous word which appears in the text, *tuhall*; then, somehow, he ended up writing *tudāf*, 'mix', which appears in his printed text.

Chapter X

Khushkanānaj. Chelebi incorporated 'and let the almonds be half as much as the sugar' from *Minhāj*.

Urnīn. Chelebi informed Arberry he believed the correct form of this word to be *bādhīn*, but it appears in the other medieval cookbooks as *urnīn*.

Ruṭab Muᶜassal. Here Chelebi (or perhaps the later editor al-Barudi) changed *al-gharīq* to *al-farīq* 'band, party, detachment'.

Ṣifat ᶜamal ruṭab fī ghair awānihi. *Battīkhat raqqī* has been changed (but perhaps only in al-Barudi's edition) to *battīkha raqqiyya*. In Iraq, where *raqqī* (now pronounced *raggī*) is the word for watermelon, it is a noun, not an adjective.

(**Hais**. Al-Barudi has 'half or a quarter of a pound' instead of 'a half and a quarter of a pound'.)

Shawābīr. Chelebi plausibly read *mudaww* as *mudawwar* 'round', as did the scribe of the London MS. (In *K. Waṣf* it is 'a tinned copper' pan.)

Ṣifat ᶜamal al-Kabula. Chelebi read *qalīlan* 'a little' as *qalīlan qalīlan* 'little by little'.

APPENDIX II

THIS TRANSLATION AND ARBERRY'S COMPARED

Terms used in more than one recipe:

'A while': Arberry always translates *sāᶜa* as 'hour'. In a very few recipes such as *Fustuqiyya* it does appear to mean an hour, and there I translate it as such. In every other case it means 'a while', a non-specific length of time which is often explained by a phrase beginning 'until'. It is quite impossible for it to mean 'an hour' in, e.g., *nāranjiyya*, where meatballs are dipped in egg yolk and returned to the pot to cook 'for a *ṣāᶜa*', and the process is repeated three more times.

'Mixed spices': following Chelebi, Arberry misread *aṭrāf al-ṭīb* ('sides of scent') as *aẓfār al-ṭīb*, i.e. *blattes de Bysance*, the fragrant operculum of a certain marine snail. As other medieval cookbooks show, *aṭrāf al-ṭīb* meant mixed spices, the equivalent of modern Arab mixtures such as *ḥawāyij* and *bahārāt*.

'Meatballs': Arberry translated *kubab* and *kubāb* as 'cabobs'. Since they are always made of ground meat and thrown into stew, and in the sweetmeats section they are a shape, '(meat)balls' is a better translation.

'To stew': Arberry translated the verb *ᶜarraqa* literally as 'to cause (something) to sweat', understanding it to mean frying meat until it exudes its moisture. Sometimes *ᶜarraqa* does seem just a synonym for frying. In *aruzz mufalfal*, meat is first fried, then boiled, and after all the water evaporates it starts to sweat: that is, to fry in the rendered fat of the meat. However, 'to sweat' cannot be the culinary meaning of this word, because sometimes meat is entirely covered with water and then 'sweated'. For that matter, Arberry quoted Reinhardt Dozy's observation that *ᶜarraqa* is applied to 'cooking [dry figs] in water, with a view to preserving them'. Arberry translated this verb in various other ways as well: 'to be juicy', 'to give off its juices' and (often in Chapter III) 'to fry lightly'.

One thing is clear about *ᶜarraqa*: it describes a preliminary or at most an intermediary step of cooking; never a final one. After the sweating, there is always another phase on the fire before the dish is done. The book's introduction points out that sweating before boiling is characteristic of the dishes called *sawādhij* and *qalāyā*, and that it is a way of preventing the rise of a scum (of congealed blood) when the meat is later boiled. Perhaps this was the original sense of the verb – to 'sweat away' the potential scum. I have chosen to render *ᶜarraqa* as 'to stew'; not a perfect translation, I am aware, but more idiomatic than 'to sweat'.

'Soy sauce': *murrī* was made by rotting barley according to exact instructions which produce a liquid sauce that tastes quite like soy sauce; a recipe is given at the end of the book. Arberry left the word *murrī* untranslated, and he misunderstood the recipe because he read the rare word *fūdhaj* ('rotted') as a variant of *fūdhīnaj*, 'pennyroyal'.

Arberry's 'beet' is *silq*, 'Swiss chard'. Arab cooks prefer to use the fleshy stalks, rather than the green leafy portion.

'Sour'/'bitter': in *baṣaliyya* and *safarjaliyya*, Arberry translated *ḥāmiḍ/muḥammaḍa* 'sour/soured' as 'bitter'. In fact, al-Baghdādī refers to bitterness only once: when olives are salted (in *zaitūn mubakhkhar*) to remove it. Oddly, Arberry translates this 'until the sourness passes off'!

'Quarter lengthwise': fleshy vegetables like the eggplant were generally split lengthwise in four parts before cooking, using two cuts that, on end, form a cross (*ṣalīb*). *Ṣalīb* can also mean 'hard' or 'firm', which led Arberry to translations like 'splitting the eggplant thoroughly'.

'Lean meat': in Arabic, *laḥm aḥmar* 'red meat' does not contrast with white meat, such as chicken, but with fat meat (*laḥm samīn*).

'Whole raw eggs': *ᶜuyūn al-baiḍ*, 'eyes of eggs', refers to eggs which are cooked with the yolks unbroken (so that they resemble eyes). Generally in this book they are cooked on the surface of a stew. Arberry translated this term as 'poached eggs'.

'Linen': Arberry consistently read *kittān*, 'linen', as 'cotton'.

'Beat sweet almonds fine and pound to a liquid consistency with water': Arberry generally translates this frequent instruction as 'sweet almonds are chopped fine and moistened (or soaked) in water'. The nuts are pounded (*madqūq*), not chopped. Such instructions are intended to make a nut-based liquid for thickening a sauce; in effect, almond milk, though apparently without straining out the solid residue of the almonds.

'Jujubes' are often rendered as 'raisins', Arberry evidently reading *ᶜunnāb* 'jujubes' as *ᶜinab* 'grapes'.

'Sour grapes': sweet grapes are not used in this book, only sour grapes (*ḥiṣrim*). Arberry translates this word sometimes as 'grapes', sometimes as 'raisins'.

'Celery leaves': during the Middle Ages, only the leaves of the celery plant were eaten, hence instructions like 'celery cut from its roots and stems'.

'Date molasses': Arberry's 'date-juice' or 'date-honey' was *dibs*, a thick treacle or molasses of boiled down juice of dates (or other sweet things, such as grapes or carob).

The word *bāqāt* means 'bundles, bunches'. When it refers to herbs, Arberry translated it as 'sprigs', rather plausibly. But 'sprigs' of spinach or chard is quite absurd, so I have translated this word as 'bunches', agnostic as to their size.

'To milk (nuts) with water' (*yustaḥlab*): in *nīrbāj* and *isfīdhabāja*, Arberry translated this 'to stir in water'.

Arberry's 'beans' are *bāqillā*, broad beans, known in America as fava beans. His 'pulse' is *māsh*, mung beans or Bengal gram.

Arberry translated both *ᶜūd dārṣīnī* (a stick of Chinese cinnamon, viz. *Cinnamomum aromaticum*) and *ᶜīdān dārṣīnī* (sticks of cinnamon) as 'cinnamon bark'.

'Cloves of garlic': several times in Chapter VII, Arberry translates *asnān thūm*, 'cloves (literally, teeth) of garlic', as 'quarters of garlic'.

Arberry consistently read *nāᶜima* as 'soft', but in Chapter IX it has the sense of 'smooth' when applied to the smooth floor tile ('soft surface') used as a pastry marble and the head of the iron peg ('iron stake with a soft head') used for stretching candies.

In Chapters VIII and IX Arberry began to translate *dist*, which he had earlier rendered as 'a copper bowl' (in the recipe for *Bādhinjān Maḥsī* on page 87), as 'dish'. From *Makshūfa* to the end of Chapter XI it becomes 'a basin'.

Introduction

'The resurrector of mankind': Arberry's reading 'he hath brought every creature to life' is what we should expect an introduction to say, but the text has *munashshir al-anām*. Arberry may have read *mubshir*, associating it with a verb meaning 'to bring forth vegetation' (of the earth) or *bashar*, 'human being'.

'Who with His manifest blessings causes the plants to grow which encompass the land': Arberry read *barriyya* (land, countryside) as *bariyya* (creation) and translated this '(He) has made herbs to grow; and He encompasseth all mankind with His manifold blessings'.

‘Those which a forbidden thing has not contaminated’: since the vowels were not written in the published Arabic text, Arberry read *lam yashubhu muḥarram* as *lam yushabbah muḥarram*, ‘that it be not doubtful or unlawful’ (literally, ‘that a proscribed thing not be doubtful’)

‘(It is not forbidden) to be meticulous about (food)’: here Arberry translated *ta*ʾ*annuq* as ‘to take delight in’, but two sentences later he translated the same verb as ‘(which) he had prepared to the best of his ability’.

Chapter I

Al-Sikbāj. ‘Its scum and froth’: ‘the froth and cream’, Arberry perhaps reading *zabaduhu* ‘its froth’ as *zubda* ‘butter’.

Ibrāhīmiyya. ‘galingale’: Arberry did not translate the word *ʿūd*, perhaps because its more usual meaning ‘a stick’ suggested that it was a measure of ginger.

‘without boiling’: ‘without skinning’. (But the verb *salaqa* can indeed mean ‘to remove the skin by boiling’.)

Jurjāniyya. ‘carrots from which the woody interior has been removed, chopped medium’: ‘walnuts, first shelling and them chopping up into middling pieces’. Here the error is al-Baghdādī’s; the London MS corrected *jauz* ‘walnuts’ to *jazar* ‘carrots’.

‘pomegranates and black raisins in equal proportion (*niṣfain bil-sawā*)’: ‘pomegranates and black grapes cut in halves’.

Dīkabrīka. ‘mix with rose-water and vinegar’: Arberry omits ‘with’, as if these two liquids are merely mixed together, rather than with the ground almonds and other ingredients preceding.

Nīrbāj. ‘small or medium’: ‘middling pieces’.

‘If you like to put in carrots’: ‘and leeks if desired’.

‘a third as much of black raisins’: ‘a third the quantity

of the seeds of black grapes'. (The preceding ingredient is pomegranate seeds, which at most seasons of the year were a dried ingredient and had to be pounded, macerated and strained to be usable. Arberry took 'seeds' to refer to the grapes as well and the seeds themselves to be the ingredient, not the dried fruit around them; hence he translated 'pound' in the following instruction as 'grind'.)

'When the meat stews and the water decreases, sprinkle lean meat with spices': 'While the meat is stewing, and its juices are being given off, mince up red meat with seasonings'.

Ṭabāhaja. Arberry suggests that 'sliced meat' refers to slicing it from the bone, but the following instruction says to 'slice' tail fat. It seems the medieval practice was to cut meat into slices (*sharāʾiḥ*) and then to cut them into smaller pieces.

Ḥulwiyya. 'carrots': 'leeks', again.

'small pieces of sweet prunes': Arberry read this ambiguously spelled passage as *qitaᶜ mubaḥthara wa ḥalwā al-qurāḍiyya* 'pieces of *mubaḥthara* and *qurāḍiyya*' (two pastries, one of them speculative), and he consequently read the name of the dish as *ḥalawiyya*, deriving it from *ḥalwā*. However, the text clearly spells the name *ḥulwiyya*, and I interpret the passage as *qiṭaᶜ yasīra (min) ḥulw al-qarāṣiyā*, which is in line with the London MS, *K. Wasf* and *ḥulwiyya* recipes in other books, all of which are sweetened with dried fruits.

Rummāniyya. 'take sour pomegranates, strip them by hand and squeeze them well': 'take sour pomegranates, squeeze very well in the hand'.

Rībāsiyya. 'rhubarb': 'redcurrants'. Perhaps Arberry was thinking of *Ribes*, the botanical name of the redcurrant.

Līmūniyya: *Līmūīwiya*.

Mishmishiyya: 'macerate by hand': 'wipe in the hands'.

Nāranjiyya. 'Take safflower (seeds)': 'take cardamom-seeds'. Safflower (*qurṭum*) seeds were milked in water just like almonds and walnuts.

Chapter II

[c]**Adasiyya**. The passage 'When the chard is done, add the necessary amount of water. Then boil it' was omitted by Arberry.

Ḥinṭiyya. 'bruise it a little in the mortar': *turaḍḍ yasīran* might also be read Arberry's way, 'crush it fine in the mortar'.

Sughdiyya. 'let them be hot so that the whites coat them and stick to them': 'let them be hot so as to absorb the whites and be covered by them'.

Chapter III

Al-[c]Anbariyya. 'macerate it by hand. Press out its juice': 'dry it by hand, squeezing out the water'.

'dry it on a tray (*ṭabaq*)': 'serve dry in a dish'.

Safarjaliyya. 'sour ripe quinces': 'ripe, bitter quince'.

Mudaqqaqāt ḥāmiḍa. This is another of the places where Arberry misread *ḥāmiḍa* 'sour' as 'bitter'.

'When it is done and casts off its fat': 'When cooked, remove the oils'.

Būrān. 'beat them well with a ladle until they become like a pudding': 'beat well with a ladle, until it becomes like *kabīṣ*'. The consistency is of a flour-thickened pudding (*khabīṣ*), not the stew *kabīṣ*.

Manbūsha. 'tendons and cartilage': 'veins and gristle'. Since there is no way to remove veins from meat, I interpret *[c]urūq* ('roots, veins') as tendons.

Madfūna. 'remove all that fills its interior': Arberry read *bizrihi*, 'its seeds', but the text explicitly spells this word *bazrihi*, 'that which fills it'.

Būrāniyyat al-Qar[c]. 'onions in proportion to the meat': 'onion as required'.

Ruṭabiyya. Perhaps Arberry read *gharīq(an)* as *ᶜarīq*, 'deeply rooted; noble', to arrive at his translation 'take sugarcandy dates, or Medina dates'. This reading is made less plausible by the fact that in al-Baghdādī's text the adjective is in the accusative case, which implies that it specifies a condition ('when they are drowned'), rather than the name of a variety of date.

Khashkhāshiyya. 'Sprinkle it with half a *dirham* of salt': 'drop in half a *dirham*', omitting the salt.

ᶜUnnābiyya. Again I translate *ᶜurūq* as tendons, not veins.

Chapter IV

Harīsa. 'Then beat it again': 'then stir again'.

Akāriᶜ. 'Take the trotters from a year-old lamb': 'Take a yearling lamb'. Because the instruction *al-akāriᶜ tuttakhad min ḥamal ḥaulī* appears after the title **Akāriᶜ**, Arberry assumed it was a dittography, and as a result he put the whole lamb in the pot.

Chapter V

Muṭajjan. 'Take a suckling kid and scald it': 'Take suckling kid, skin'.

'Dry it after boiling': 'After scalding, dry'.

Ṣifa ukhrā, nāshifa. 'Boil a jointed kid in vinegar': 'Cut a kid into quarters, and scald in vinegar'.

'boil it in vinegar': 'scald in water'. In both these passages, the verb is *yuslaq* 'boil', not *yusmat* 'scald'.

Maṣūṣ. 'Take a suckling kid, scald it and cut it up into joints': 'Take a suckling kid and skin, cut into quarters'.

'When it (viz. the celery leaf) stews, throw the kid in the pot': 'When the kid is juicy (Sc. after frying in the oil), place it in the saucepan'.

Maqlūba. ‘a thin (*laṭīf*) iron or copper pan’: ‘a fine iron or copper frying-pan’.

Bazmāward. ‘Take excellent pithy *samīd* bread and remove its crumb. Then stuff it well with that roast meat’ (*yuḥshā min dhālika al-shiwāʾ ḥashwan jayyidan*): ‘Take good pithy white bread, extract the pith, and with this stuff the roast well’. As shown by other medieval recipes, *bazmāward* was a sort of sandwich or canape, not roast meat stuffed with bread crumbs.

Baiḍ Maṣūṣ. Arberry omitted the instruction ‘When they fry (*yuṭajjan*)’.

Chapter VI

Samak Mashwī. The roasting spit is ‘of iron’ (*ḥadīd*), not ‘new’ (*jadīd*).

‘Cover its top (long) enough that it is known that it is done’: ‘Cover, and leave to cook well’.

Māliḥ Nāʿim. ‘make delicate slashes in it (the fish)’: ‘make small holes [in the fish]’. The Arabic is *yushaqqu fīhi shuqūqan diqāqan*.

Samak Maqlū bi-Khall wa-Rahshī. ‘If you like, put a little finely pounded mustard in it, and it might be made with other (flavourings) than that’: ‘If desired, some fine-ground mustard may be added, but this is not necessary’. Arberry interpreted the ambiguous phrase *bi-ghair dhālika* as ‘without that’, but since mustard was explicitly introduced as an optional flavouring, I prefer to entertain the sense ‘with other than that’.

Māliḥ bi-Laban. ‘Take salted fish, wash it and cut it as we have described’: ‘Take salted fish, wash and clean as described’. I have no doubt that in this recipe *laban* is yogurt, rather than milk, as Arberry translated it.

Maqlūbat al-Ṭarrīkh. ‘pick their bones and spines clean – pick them extremely well, as well as you can': 'bone, and scale with the greatest care'. The verb is the same in both phrases (*yunaqqā/tanqiya*), and it seems to refer to removing the meat (which is further processed in the next step), rather than the scales.

Mufarraka. 'like *mufarraka*, which has been mentioned before': 'as in making *mufarraka* [recte *maqlūba*] as described above'. The difference between the two dishes is that *maqlūba* is an egg cake which is fried on both sides, *mufarraka* is a scramble which is stirred as it cooks. This dish does indeed brown like the *mufarraka* in Chapter V, not like the *maqlūba* previous.

Chapter VII

Lift Mukhallal Muḥallā. 'As for (the kind) that is not sweetened, cut them up': 'What is not dissolved may be cut up'. Chelebi changed al-Baghdādī's *lam yuḥallā*, 'not sweetened', to the grammatically correct spelling *lam yuḥall*(*a*), and Arberry read this as *lam yuḥall*, 'not dissolved'.

'As for smooth cucumbers, ridged cucumbers, onions and other (vegetables) which you want to pickle, put them in vinegar alone until they soften and mature': 'For sousing cucumber, capers, onion and the like, put into vinegar as required, leave until soft and tender'. The instruction distinguishes between two kinds of cucumber, *khiyār* and *quththāʾ*; Arberry read the last as *qubbār*, 'capers'. He read *ḥasb* as *ḥasaba* 'according to' with an omitted object such as *al-ḥāja*; I take it as equivalent to *fa-ḥasb* 'and no more, only', meaning that these vegetables are pickled in vinegar alone, without spices and herbs.

Bādhinjān bi-Laban. Again I think *laban* must mean yogurt, rather than fresh milk.

'Refine fresh sesame oil with a bit of cumin and coriander and throw it on it. Sprinkle a bit of mixed spices and nigella (*shūnīz*) on it': 'Refine fresh sesame-oil, add a little cumin and coriander, and into this place the eggplant. Sprinkle with some *blattes de Bysance* and sesame'.

Qar^c bi-Laban. 'Persian yogurt': 'Persian milk'.

Silq bi-Laban. 'Persian yogurt': 'Persian milk'.

'nigella': 'sesame'.

Shīrāz bi-Buqūl. '*shīrāz*': 'dried curds'.

'renneted yogurt (*al-laban al-mās*)': 'coagulated milk'.

'sour yogurt': 'sour milk'.

Kāmakh Rījāl. 'Dry red rose petals': 'dried leaves of the red rose'.

Zaitūn Mubakhkhar. The recipe makes it clear that the meaning of *mubakhkhar* is literally 'smoked', not 'perfumed'.

'until their bitterness goes away': 'until the sourness passes off'.

'Then put them on a tray woven of sticks (*^calā ṭabaq min ^cīdān mushabbak*)': 'Put grated cinnamon on a plate'. Arberry clearly read *^cīdān* 'sticks' as sticks of cinnamon; the source of 'grated' is hard to see. Later he translates *al-ṭabaq al-mushabbak* as 'the reticulated plate'.

'Put that on it': 'then add to the cinnamon'.

Milḥ Muṭayyab. 'The salt might be coloured (*wa-qad yuṣbagh al-milḥ*)': 'colour it'. Arberry missed the particle *qad* in this passage but noted it in the later instruction on colouring the salt with sumac or vermilion.

Bāqillā bi-Khall: *Bāquili bī-Khall.*

Chapter VIII.

Jūdhāb al-Khubz. 'soak it in water or fresh milk until it sours [until it grows (matures); *Minhāj*]': 'soak in water or fresh milk until moist'. Both manuscripts of al-Baghdādī and the identical recipes that appear in *Kitāb Wasf* and the contemporary *Kitāb al-Wuṣla ilā al-Ḥabīb* say to soak the bread until it sours (*ḥattā yakhtamir*). However, Chelebi preferred the marginal note from the *Minhāj*, *ḥattā yarbū*, which Arberry read as 'until it is moist', perhaps connecting it with the word *rubb*, 'thickened fruit juice, pulp'.

Jūdhāb al-Qaṭāyif. 'Take fried crepes stuffed with almonds and sugar': 'Take *qaṭāʾif* stuffed with almonds and sugar and fried'.

Ṣifa ukhrā. 'stir it with a poker until the fat is released': 'stirring with a poker until the oil is resolved'.

Ṣifa ukhrā. 'put a pound of toasted *samīd* flour on it': 'crumble into it a *raṭl* of white meal'.

'stir it with the poker until it casts off its fat, and take it up': 'stirring with a poker, until the oil comes away and is thrown off'.

Chapter IX

Ḥalwā Yābisa. Arberry says to 'plant' (*yuḍrab*, 'beat') the peg (or stake) in the sugar mass, but, as other recipes show, it was instead pounded into a wall for stretching the candy.

'Some of it might be rolled (or kneaded)': 'Sometimes it is crumbled'.

Ṣābūniyya. 'dissolve sugar, then take it from the *dist* and put it in a vessel. Then throw sesame oil (into the *dist*), and when it boils, throw some of the syrup on it': 'Dissolve sugar, then pour it out of the dish into a vessel, adding sesame-oil; when boiling, throw in some syrup'. Arberry has both sugar and sesame in the vessel (*ināʾ*), leaving the boiling unexplained.

Makshūfa. 'so that it boils (*yaghlī*) and boils up (*yafūr*)': 'and boil until fragrant'. Did Arberry mistake *yafūr* for *yafūḥ*?

Lauzīnaj. 'roll it up like a belt' (*yuṭwā kal-sair*): 'fold round strip-wise'.

Fālūdhaj. '*ausāṭ*': 'middling pieces'.

Mukaffan: '*ausāṭ*': 'belts'.

Barad. 'Take the necessary amount of sugar, dissolve it with rose-water': 'Take honey as required, and mix with rose-water'.

Samak wa-Aqrāṣ. 'dissolve an ounce of starch in rose-water': 'Mix an uqiya of starch with rose-water'.

Chapter X

Khushkanānaj. In this and other pastry recipes, Arberry speculated that 'gathering' refers to impressing patterns on them with carved moulds, which is possible; but cf. *urnīn* below, where 'gathering' (*tujma*^{c}) and 'stamping' (*tukhtam*) appear to be separate operations.

Urnīn wa-Khubz al-Abāzīr. 'let there be a mould for them like a box' (*kal-ḥuqq*): 'using an appropriate mould' (*kal-haqq*; 'like what is due'). Both readings are possible.

'four ounces of sesame oil and half a *rub*^{c} of peeled sesame seed': 'four *ūqiya* of sesame-oil and an eighth of this quantity of shelled sesame'. *Rub*^{c} is an ambiguous measure; it literally means 'a quarter', and it can refer to a quarter of a *dirham* (= $^{3}/_{4}$ gram) or a quarter of any given measurement, but here I believe it means a quarter of a *qadaḥ*, or about one measuring cup.

NB: Although Arberry does not note it, this recipe calls for a European-type bread oven (*furn*) rather than the tandoor (*tannūr*) called for in other chapters.

Aqrāṣ Mukallala. 'Cover them with that dough' (*yulbas bi-dhālika al-*^{c}*ajīn*): 'spread over that dough'.

Ruṭab Mu^{c}assal. 'until the weather is cold and it enters the Kānūns (December and January)': 'until the weather is cold and chafing-dishes are brought in'. Against Arberry's interpretation, the text spells the verb in the active voice. *K. Waṣf* has a clearer instruction: 'Use them only during the chilly season, and when the fresh date season is over'.

In this recipe Arberry left the puzzling word *gharīq/farīq* untranslated.

Ṣifat ᶜamal ruṭab fī ghair awānihi. 'large dried dates': 'poor quality dates'. Arberry read *qaṣb*, 'dry dates that crumble in the mouth' as *quṣāb*, 'poor quality dates'.

'spikenard': 'hyacinth'.

Ṣifat ᶜamal al-Kabūlā. 'moisten it with a little sesame oil, about an ounce': 'pour in an *ūqiya* of sesame oil, little by little'.